Beyond
THE SILK ROAD

❖ arts of Central Asia ❖

FROM THE POWERHOUSE MUSEUM COLLECTION

by Christina Sumner

POWERHOUSE PUBLISHING
PART OF THE MUSEUM OF APPLIED ARTS AND SCIENCES

First published 1999
Powerhouse Publishing, Sydney

Powerhouse Publishing
part of the Museum of Applied Arts and Sciences
PO Box K346 Haymarket NSW 1238 Australia
The Museum of Applied Arts and Sciences incorporates the
Powerhouse Museum and Sydney Observatory.

Project management: Julie Donaldson, Powerhouse Museum
Editing: Rowena Lennox
Design: Peter Thorn, i2i design
Photography: Powerhouse Museum Photography Section – Sotha Bourn,
Penelope Clay, Marinco Kojdanovski and Sue Stafford
Printing: Inprint Pty Ltd
Typeset in Calligraphic, Helvetica Neue and Perpetua

The authors wish to thank Cito and Lyn Cessna, Ross and Irene Langlands
and Suzanne Pennell for so generously sharing their expertise and knowledge
of Central Asian material culture with us; Christina Hargreave for her
invaluable assistance with research and pictorial coordination; and the
Cadry family for their encouragement and support.

National Library of Australia CIP
Sumner, Christina
Beyond the Silk Road: arts of Central Asia
from the Powerhouse Collection
ISBN 1 8317 069 3
1. Art, Central Asian. I Feltham, Heleanor B
II. Title
709.58

Published in conjunction with the exhibition *Beyond the Silk Road: arts of
Central Asia* at the Powerhouse Museum 30 August 1999 – June 2000.
Distributed by Bookwise International (Australia and NZ) and Lund Humphries (UK, USA and other territories).

Cover image: detail of a chromolithograph of decorative painting from
Central Asia, drawn by Nicolai Simakoff in Bukhara in 1879, printed in
St Petersburg, Russia in 1882. See page 79 for full image.

Contents

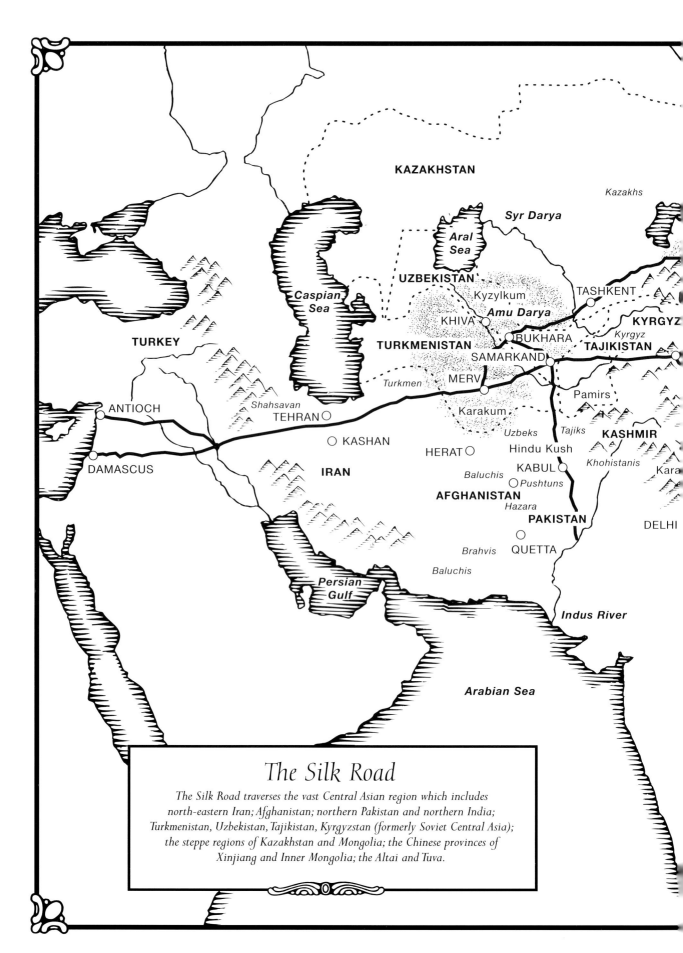

KAZAKHSTAN

Kazakhs

Syr Darya

Aral Sea

Caspian Sea

UZBEKISTAN

Kyzylkum

TASHKENT

Amu Darya

KHIVA

KYRGYZ

BUKHARA

Kyrgyz

TURKMENISTAN

TAJIKISTAN

TURKEY

SAMARKAND

Pamirs

MERV

Turkmen

Uzbeks

Tajiks

ANTIOCH

Shahsavan

Karakum

KASHMIR

TEHRAN

Khohistanis

Kara

KASHAN

HERAT

Hindu Kush

DAMASCUS

Baluchis

KABUL

IRAN

Pushtuns

AFGHANISTAN

Hazara

PAKISTAN

DELHI

QUETTA

Brahvis

Baluchis

Persian Gulf

Indus River

Arabian Sea

The Silk Road

*The Silk Road traverses the vast Central Asian region which includes
north-eastern Iran; Afghanistan; northern Pakistan and northern India;
Turkmenistan, Uzbekistan, Tajikistan, Kyrgyzstan (formerly Soviet Central Asia);
the steppe regions of Kazakhstan and Mongolia; the Chinese provinces of
Xinjiang and Inner Mongolia; the Altai and Tuva.*

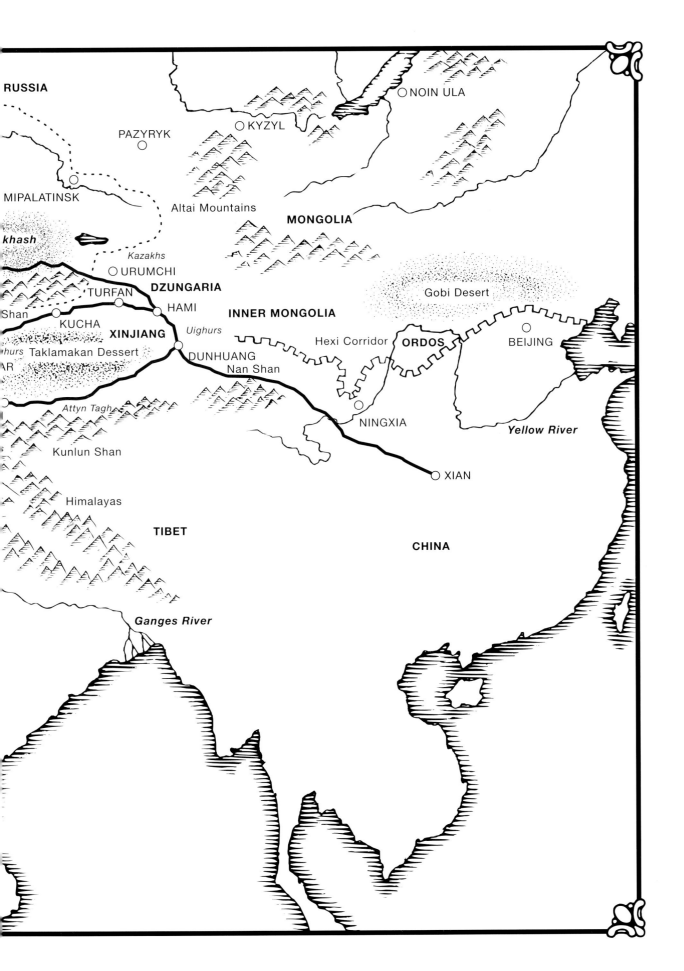

RUSSIA

PAZYRYK

MIPALATINSK

khash

Kazakhs

URUMCHI

DZUNGARIA

Shan

TURFAN

HAMI

KUCHA

XINJIANG

Uighurs

hurs Taklamakan Dessert

AR

DUNHUANG

Nan Shan

Attyn Tagh

Kunlun Shan

Himalayas

TIBET

Ganges River

KYZYL

NOIN ULA

Altai Mountains

MONGOLIA

INNER MONGOLIA

Gobi Desert

Hexi Corridor

ORDOS

BEIJING

NINGXIA

Yellow River

XIAN

CHINA

Director's foreword

Beyond the Silk Road: arts of Central Asia has been published in association with the exhibition of the same name in the Powerhouse Museum's Asian Gallery. The exhibition and the book, both designed to make the museum's collection widely accessible, explore the symbiotic relationship between the nomadic and urban peoples of Central Asia through carpets, textiles, dress and other objects produced by them.

The Powerhouse museum holds Australia's largest collection of textiles and dress, and a significant collection of Asian decorative arts and design, both of which have developed steadily since the museum's genesis in 1879. This exhibition draws substantively on the museum's Central Asian collection, and displays for the first time a group of chromolithographs acquired during the museum's first five years in accordance with its earliest acquisition policies.

With the dissolution of the Soviet Union, world interest has turned increasingly towards Central Asia, the spotlight falling in particular on the five newly-independent republics of Kazakstan, Kyrgyzstan, Tajikistan, Turkmenistan and Uzbekistan that comprise western Central Asia. The extraordinarily rich history of this region, its contemporary significance, and the pivotal role its inhabitants played both upon the Silk Road and beyond are now receiving growing recognition. *Beyond the Silk Road: arts of Central Asia* constitutes a timely contribution by the museum to the field of Central Asian studies.

I would like to thank Dr Brian Kennedy and Robyn Maxwell of the National Gallery of Australia for making objects from their Central Asian collection available to us for loan for the exhibition; three of those objects are reproduced in this publication. I would also like to thank the Oriental Rug Society of NSW for its valuable support for the museum over many years.

I would also like to acknowledge the many staff who have contributed to this publication and to the development of the exhibition. In particular, I wish to thank Christina Sumner for initiating and coordinating this project, and Heleanor Feltham who has worked closely with her on all aspects of the project.

Terence Measham AM
Director, Powerhouse Museum, Sydney

Introduction

Christina Sumner and Heleanor Feltham

> The nomad must depend upon the agriculturalist for his grain, the town dweller
> looks to the nomad to provide him with horses for riding and camels for transport.
> Chinese competency in the banking business … is universally recognised, while the
> native of Turkestan is relied on for the quickest transport … Tibetan and
> Mongolian hunters supply furs which enable all to face the bitter cold of the
> Central Asian winter. By means of the hardy traffickers of the Himalayan passes,
> Indian produce such as precious stones, silk scarves, muslins and laces for women's
> veils are exchanged for Kashgarian carpets and rugs, and the artist craftsmen from
> Peking, seeking jade, depend on the rough Khotan 'jade-fishers' to fetch it from
> the bed of the river.
>
> Mildred Cable with Francesca French, *The Gobi Desert*, Hodder & Stoughton, London, 1942

The Silk Road ran from China in the east to Iran (then known as Persia) and the Mediterranean civilisations in the west—and back—passing through the cities and kingdoms of Central Asia, crossing mountain ranges through passes so high that only those with adapted lungs could safely pass, trekking deserts where phantom caravans sounded among the endless dunes, passing through rich grasslands where nomadic tribespeople preyed on undefended caravans and cities whose names echo in the mind: Herat, Tashkent, Kashgar, Khiva . . .

Never, in truth, a single route, the Silk Road branched, wandered, and rejoined itself, taking one path in good seasons when the mountain passes were clear and the oases provided abundant grass for the horses and camels, taking another when bitter cold closed the high trails or when scarcity meant the tribes were banding together for raids and incursions. Integral, too, in that vast network of exchange were the branch roads that ran north to Russia or south to the kingdoms of India.

Long after the great days of international Silk Road trade had passed—disrupted as they were by wars, the encroaching desert, and the discovery of new and quicker maritime trade routes—the pattern of local interchange continued. The nomadic and urban peoples of Central Asia maintained their mutually dependent lifestyles, marketing their beautiful carpets, embroideries and silks, both within their own domains and to an international clientele, who have never lost their fascination with the golden road to Samarkand.

By placing the Silk Road as backdrop and locating it within the context of the rich and frequently violent history of Central Asia, with its glorious artistic legacy, we can see more clearly and with greater understanding the artistic achievements of the people of Central Asia in more recent times. In our imagination, we can move with the nomads and their animals across steppes and desert, warmed as they were by the soft wool and rich colours of their rugs and trappings, and perhaps gain some insight into their love of the nomadic life. We can jostle for position in court, meetings and marketplace with the men of the towns, cloaked in the brilliant colour and sensuous luxury of urban silks. We can experience an echo of Timur's Samarkand, whose architectural marvels were built 600 years ago with massive cost in human suffering, in the delicacy of Islamic tile patterns drawn by a Russian artist, Nicolai Simakoff, in 1879.

Two and a half thousand years have elapsed between the days of the passage of the first caravans along the Silk Road, through the heartland of Asia, and today's post-Soviet world of international oil diplomacy. During those many centuries, the material culture of the Central Asian people—nomadic, semi-nomadic and oasis dwelling—has developed in response to practical and aesthetic human needs, and changed in response to internal pressures and external influences, most recently that of Tsarist and then Soviet Russia. Although most nomads were settled long ago in towns and villages, and the distinction between nomads and town dwellers in Central Asia is progressively less clear, both ways of life—pastoral and agrarian—are nevertheless reflected in the surviving material culture. In the newly independent Central Asian states of Kazakhstan, Kyrgyzstan, Tajikistan, Turkmenistan and Uzbekistan, the lives and contemporary craft production of the oasis dwellers and those who cling tenaciously to nomadic life continue to be enriched and influenced by the great arts of the past.

A brief overview of Central Asian history

Heleanor Feltham

The Central Asian region

Geographically, Central Asia consists of a great sweep
of plain—running from Pacific Ocean Siberia to the plains
of central Europe—split and walled by mountain chains,
and edged with tundra and desert. The foothills, plateaus
and valleys are verdant, often luxuriant, and support
villages, towns and (traditionally) city-states. River systems,
before they vanish into the deserts, provide water for the
occasional oasis city. Beyond the mountains, to the south,
east and west, lie the great cultural centres of the world
—India, China, Iran (Persia), Europe—reached often with
great difficulty through well-defended mountain passes or
across deserts such as the Gobi.

At the centre of the land mass, where seven countries
meet, is a great knot of mountains centring on the Pamirs.
The Hindu Kush run down through Afghanistan, the
Karakoram define Kashmir, the Himalayas, Altun Shan and
Qilian Shan border Tibet, while the Tien Shan run up through
Tajikistan, Uzbekistan, Kyrgyzstan and Xinjiang to circle the Tarim Basin (Tarim Pendi) and
the Taklimakan Desert. Beyond the Dzungarian Gap (Junggar Pendi), a further range, the Altai,
splits Mongolia from the steppes of Kazakhstan.

*Tekke Turkmen with
decorated horse outside
a yurt, before 1890.*

Photo courtesy Museum für
Völkerkunde, Vienna

The mountains give rise to river systems which, on the Central Asian side, either terminate
in inland lakes such as the Aral Sea and Lake Balkhash, or lose themselves in deserts such as the
Taklimakan. The fertile riverine and upland areas, running in an arc from Iran to China, gave rise
to a network of autonomous kingdoms centring on the so-called Silk Road oasis cities. The relative
small agriculturally viable regions supported cultures characterised by skills in farming, gardening
and irrigation (such as the Uigurs and Uzbeks).

Linked by trade and religious beliefs, the commerce between these cities transmitted and
sometimes transformed the goods and ideas of the major civilisations to the east, south and west.
From the fifth century BCE (before the common era) to the Arab conquests of the eighth century
CE (common era), these kingdoms included Chorasmia (the Transcaucasus region, now largely
Turkmenistan); Bactria (northern Afghanistan); Soghdia, between the Oxus (Amu Darya) and
Jaxartes (Syr Darya) rivers (Uzbekistan); Fergana (Tajikistan and Uzbekistan); and Kashgaria
(Xinjiang). These were home to the great Silk Road cities of Nisa, Merv, Samarkand, Piandjikent,
Bamyan, Hadda, Taxila, Kashgar, and Khotan, Kizil and Turfan.

To the north of the fertile region the land becomes increasingly arid, drying out into deserts such as the Karakumy, Taklamakan and Gobi. Beyond these, two vast steppe regions, divided by the Altai and Tien Shan mountain ranges, cover the heart of Eurasia from the Pacific Ocean through to Hungary, and include Mongolia, Inner Mongolia and Kazakhstan. This is marginal landscape, unsuited to farming, and only became viable for human settlement with the development of mounted nomadism during the third millennium BCE. Nomadism as a way of life allowed the seasonal movement of people and their meat animals from uplands to lowlands or from one grazing ground to the next.

The origins and traditional arts of the nomads

The proto-Turkic and Indo-European horse-breeding peoples of Central Asia developed a way of life which was first described by the Greek historian Herodotus (484–425? BCE) and by the Chinese historian Sima Quian (145–86 BCE), who wrote respectively about the Scythians and the Xiongnu (Huns). The lifestyle, which remains relatively unchanged even today, involved the seasonal movement of herds of, mainly, sheep, horses and camels, often over vast areas (the Scythians are recorded as trading with the Greeks in the Black Sea region, while their principal burial sites appear to be in the Altai Mountains). Quickly erected mobile homes (the traditional felt yurt or *gur*), and riding and baggage animals such as camels and horses were essential to this way of life.

Today's horses evolved from three Central Asian ancestors, the Asian wild horse, the forest tarpan and the steppe tarpan. The steppe tarpan ranged the Turanian plain, the snow-free pastureland around the Aral Sea, where predation from wolves and big cats ensured the development of a fast, alert, strong animal. In neolithic times, perhaps as early as 7500 BCE, horses were corralled close to the semi-nomadic settlements of the Turan to serve as live provisions. Somewhere along the line the nomads found that their dinners could be ridden. Precisely when is difficult to determine, given that the most likely riding equipment—felt blanket, leather rein, padded wool and wood saddle—is also the least likely to survive, while the arts of nomadic people are also usually transitory. Nevertheless, the oldest extant carpet, dating from the sixth century BCE, was found in the ice-tomb of a Scythian nomad buried at Pazyryk in the Altai. Around its borders are woven images of horsemen.

Turan horses were widely bred and traded both east and west of the Transcaucasus, evolving by around 1000 BCE into the Akhal-Tekke, the 'heavenly horses of Fergana' as the Chinese called them, which travelled to Greece with the Persian invasions in the early fifth century BCE, and to China with the soldiers of the Han emperor Wudi (141–86) in the second century BCE. Wudi conquered the kingdoms of the Tarim Basin and Fergana, and formally established the Silk Road, controlling Central Asian trade and introducing an infinitely superior cavalry horse into the wars against the nomadic Xiongnu.

From the initial domestication of the horse as a riding animal to the Manchu conquest of China in 1644 CE, the nomads of Central Asia have interacted, often violently, with the cultures that surround them. The first wave out of the Caucasus, the Indo-Europeans, set the pattern of raids, invasion, settlement and eventual blending into the local civilisation. There were always limits on the capacity of the steppe to support its tribes, and several bad seasons could lead to a domino-effect. Most commonly, a series of bad seasons in, say, Mongolia would drive several related tribes to amalgamate, incorporating or dispossessing weaker groups. Sometimes this led to

Detail of the Pazyryk carpet showing a section of the border frieze featuring mounted horsemen. It was made about 2500 years ago and found in a Scythian tomb.

Photo courtesy The State Hermitage Museum, St Petersburg

little more than a shifting in tribal boundaries; however, when tribes became united by charismatic and expansionist leaders, such as Attila the Hun (about 406–453) or Genghis Khan (1162–1227), incursions could become conquests.

The Xiongnu migrations are a significant example. A typical Mongolian nomad tribe, they first occupied the Ordos region north-west of China in 177 BCE, driving out the Yuezhi who then migrated first to the Oxus Valley and then, around 135 BCE, settled in Bactria. Later, several tribes of the Xiongnu would themselves be driven out, one group invading northern India and one continuing through into Europe, where they were known as the Huns. The remaining Xiongnu, federating with other groups such as the Xianbi, would themselves move into a weakened China in the early fourth century CE.

In this process nomadic peoples often moved into agriculturally rich areas and became sedentary (usually through conquest and intermarriage), adding their own rich imagery and beliefs to the older cultures. Typical of these ex-nomads were the Parthians in Iran, the Kushans in India, the Seljuk and Ottoman Turkish empires in western Asia and the Manchus in China. But no matter how frequently tribes of nomads moved in, there were always other tribes to take their place on the vast pasture lands, or to settle for control of the oasis cities, establishing Central Asian kingdoms and khanates in the more fertile districts.

The relationship between oasis dweller and nomad was not inevitably violent. Generally the two ways of life were mutually interdependent. The oasis cities and villages depended on run-off waters from the mountains, channelled into elaborate irrigation systems that included long underground conduits that prevented the mountain streams from evaporating. These systems, combined with crop rotation and the careful reclamation of marginal ground, allowed for the cultivation of an astonishing range of fruits, nuts, grains and cotton, and the cultivation of mulberry trees and silkworms, but gave little scope for animal husbandry or horse-raising. Larger cities enabled craftspeople to develop ceramics, metal wares, wood-turning, the weaving and embroidery of silk and cotton, and the manufacture of elaborate carpets on upright looms.

Trade was essential to the growth and expansion of these centres, and was made possible by the establishment of villages and settlements along the relatively fertile strip between the mountains and the steppes, which were rarely more than a day's journey apart by bullock, camel or horse. (Today, the Karakoram Highway allows the same trading patterns to survive.) Though these settlements might be little more than a well, a *caravanserai* (camel motel) and a few cultivated fields, the network of roads allowed the transfer of goods from Iran to China. Major cities also provided venues for seasonal fairs, where nomads, merchants and city craftspeople could meet and exchange goods. The nomads provided livestock such as camels, horses and mules, without which trade was an impossibility, as well as wool and other yarns for carpets, leather and leather goods, meat and milk products, and some steppe-growing dye-plants

Nomads often extended their family incomes by working as guides, mercenaries and animal-handlers for the caravans, and would often cover a much greater range than the intercity routes of the merchants. They also traditionally raided the less well-protected or smaller caravans, especially those that took the route through the Dzungarian Gap between the Altai and Tien Shan mountains instead of crossing the Tarim Basin.

During times of relative peace and prosperity, direct trade also took place between the nomads and the major civilisations—Greece, China, Iran, Byzantium. At annual border-town fairs luxury items, tools, household goods and agricultural products, could be exchanged for fine horses and furs, wool and leatherwork and sometimes goods stolen in raids on caravans or distant cities. Because of the breadth of the nomad range, they acted as a means of transmitting arts and ideas from the borders of China to the heart of eastern Europe. The nomads also traded their own distinctive and very beautiful products—felt and woven rugs, jewellery for both men and women, and their decorative weapons. Their strongly rhythmic and powerful imagery often influenced the decorative arts of the settled areas. During the Han dynasty (202 BCE – 221 CE), for instance, the people of the Ordos region, who made use of the same themes of animal metamorphosis and animal combat as the Scythians of the Black Sea region, traded across the Great Wall with the Chinese. Their style became popular with the Chinese nobility and was incorporated into designs for metalwork, lacquer, textiles and jades.

Life for nomadic people is often harsh and demanding, dependent on the herds of horses, camels, goats and sheep for transport, for yarn for clothes, carpets, furnishings, even for housing, food and drink, and for hides, sinews and horn. Little or nothing can be wasted. However, wild animal attacks, bad seasons, intertribal raids or outbreaks of disease may decimate tribal livestock, reducing the group to subsistence hunting. A too-brief, or a too-long winter can also leave a community desperately short of food, and even wipe out whole tribes. Not surprisingly, most nomadic peoples, even while paying lip-service to the religions of more settled communities (usually Islam or Buddhism), continue to incorporate shamanistic beliefs into their arts and lives, with some rituals designed to propitiate natural forces and ensure a round of good seasons, and others designed to ensure the goodwill of the dead or of the tribe's totemic animals. Animals, both domestic and predatory, are respected and often accorded supernatural power. Their totemic nature is reflected in the enduring legends of the various modern nomads, as well as in the Mongol and pre-Islamic western Asian arts.

By 1400 BCE a distinctive nomadic style had emerged, found in grave sites as far apart as the Caucasus and the Ordos. From their intimate connection with the natural world, the Central Asians developed a visual vocabulary that included animal combat, zoomorphic metamorphosis, and totemic animals and birds. From their tradition of raids and intertribal conflict came the images of the hero on horseback and the enduring iconography of the royal hunt, the empowering of the hero through taking on the mana of such animals as the lion and the stag.

Since the nature of life meant that art, like everything else, had to be portable, creativity went into the production of textiles, jewellery, costumes and weapons, all of which have a relatively low long-term survival rate. Often, only metalwork survived burial, and our knowledge of other early Central Asian arts is limited to frozen burials such as those of Pazyryk (fifth century BCE) and Noin Ula (first century BCE), or desert sites such as the abandoned cities and graveyards of Xinjiang. Here, alongside the gold and bronze belt buckles found across Central Asia, woven carpets, inlaid and embroidered felts, wood carvings and even tattoos on the mummified bodies have been miraculously preserved. The felts, apart from their significance as art, are also an indication that the traditional nomad felt yurt was already in use.

Even today many of the nomadic pastoralists of the Central Asian region still use the traditional yurt—it appears

Detail of a Mushwani Baluchi rug dating from about 1900 which shows the traditional ram's head and horns motif reduced to geometric simplicity.

See page 41 for full illustration

on the modern Kyrgyz flag. The yurt is constructed of a lattice of willow-wood strips. Between five and eight sections are tied together to form a circular frame with a space for a carved wooden lintel and door. Further wooden ribs form the roof, locking into a small, circular frame at the top. Inner walls can be created from woven reeds (a Kazakh specialty) or hanging woven carpets. A special feature is the tent band, a broad woven panel stabilising the structure. The outer walls and roof are made from sections of thick felts held with woven ropes. Inside the ground is covered with felts, kilims or carpets; carved wooden boxes hold special household treasures and other goods are hung from the lattice or stored in woven bags. While any woodwork (including the doors and boxes) or ceramic objects are bought from specialist craftspeople, and travelling metalworkers supply bowls, tripods and water vessels, the women of the tribes traditionally create the textiles—tent-wall and appliqué felts, woven tent bands, knotted storage bags and carpets—with which to furnish and beautify their homes. Designs are passed down, usually from mother to daughter, and patterns can easily be ascribed to different tribes and clans.

Traditionally, women in the nomad tribes were allowed much greater freedom and communal responsibility than women in the Islamic oasis cities. Yurts and their furnishings are not only made by the women, but are also owned and transported by them. Men are often responsible for shearing and dying the wool and other yarns, but the women are the felt makers and weavers. The family as a whole benefits from the sale of surplus textiles, and the Turkmen women were and are renowned for the beauty of their carpets. However, in the Islamic cities, women were not permitted any life outside their homes (and even in their homes were often restricted to the women's courts). Felts and carpets were made by men in small-scale workshops in both villages and cities, while women's great art was that of embroidery for both costume, and wall and bedding textiles.

In spite of the considerable cultural differences between the nomadic and the oasis cultures, the people were often very closely related. As late as the 1800s, for instance, Uzbeks controlled many of the Central Asian cities supported by Turkmen mercenaries and Tajik farmers, while other Uzbeks and Turkmen continued to follow a nomadic lifestyle.

This combination of settled and nomadic tribalism seems to have had very early origins. Early historians such as Herodotus and Sima Qian, whose experience with the Scythian and Xiongnu was limited to border contacts, believed that nomads not only did not build cities, but were culturally antagonistic to a settled life. However, modern archaeological research has shown that they did, in fact, establish townships and even fortified cities in areas where agriculture could be successfully practised; several have now been excavated at both the Siberian and the Caucasian ends of the nomad range. It is probable that many of the major cities along the Silk Road were established in this way. Certainly, various waves of Mongol and Turkic peoples established their own control of neighbouring farming and pasture lands from these centres and promoted both intercity and international trade, and the development of flourishing local crafts industries.

Unfortunately, the caravans of the Silk Road and the seasonal direct trade with the rich, settled communities of, especially, China and Iran provided temptations irresistible to nomadic cultures for whom raiding and banditry were honourable activities. Border raids and incursions led to the occasional punitive expedition or active attempt to gather the nomads and the trade cities into an imperial system. Unusually aggressive leaders such as Alexander the Great (356–323 BCE) in the fourth century BCE or Wudi in the second occasionally succeeded, but it has rarely been possible to maintain control of the fiercely independent nomads for long. As late as the 1800s, the Russians discovered, when attempting to impose an imperial system of regional control on the Kazakhs, that people who can simply pack up and move away from a difficult situation are very hard to colonise. More importantly, establishing military fortresses on the steppes was next to impossible, even with modern transport and communication, given that the region is vast and not suitable for agriculture, while extending lines of supply and communications along the Silk Road trade routes was almost as difficult.

The Silk Road

The Silk Road network had been in unofficial existence for several centuries before Emperor Wudi's emissary, Zhang Qian, returned from his Central Asian journeying in 126 BCE to advise the emperor that, without imperial control, trade in Chinese silks and other goods provided no taxes. Chinese control and protection of the trading cities from Dunhuang to Fergana provided an ideal climate for the growth of trade and, even after the fall of the Han dynasty, it continued to grow. Some idea of its extent can be found in the spread of Sassanian Persian imagery in the sixth to ninth centuries CE. Figured silks woven in Iran, together with Chinese, Japanese or European copies, featuring distinctive imagery reminiscent of nomad styles (semi-abstract floral patterns, confronted animals, heraldic beasts, the royal hunt—all within the distinctive Sassanian rondel) can be found in church treasuries in Germany and France and in monastic depositories in Japan.

Silk was by no means the only commodity to travel the route. Luxury items such as Byzantine glass, Central Asian carpets, slaves, cosmetics, ivory, Indian Ocean coral and Turkmen horses; musical instruments; games such as chess and polo; wine; foods and plants such as rhubarb, peaches, peonies and almonds; ceramics; dyes and glazes; exotic animals such as peacocks, parrots and salukis; equally exotic entertainers—Indian jugglers, Persian dancers, musicians from Bactria and African acrobats; new technologies such as cogs and wheelbarrows, ironfounding, gunpowder, kites and printing; religious texts and religious refugees—Parsees, Nestorians, Buddhists all followed the same path east to west or west to east across mountains, around deserts and through stretches of grasslands.

While there were always a few dedicated priests or adventurous travellers and traders who covered great stretches of the route, on the whole, merchants travelled only relatively short distances, sometimes no more than between oasis cities. The constant interchange added greatly to the price of goods, so a relatively cheap commodity or manufactured item at its source, such as Byzantine glass or Chinese silk, could become an invaluable luxury at the far end of the exchange trail.

Key factors in determining the extent of trade and cultural exchange along the Silk Road were the strength and stability of the 'static' cultures—Mediterranean, Iranian, north Indian, and Chinese; the viability of the oasis cities and smaller watering places; and the pressures on both of the Central Asian nomads. Civilisations change their dynasties, their beliefs, their technologies and their aesthetics, but not their penchant for trade. During periods of greatest confidence and expansion, such as that of Hellenistic Greece in the third century BCE, or of Tang dynasty China in the seventh century CE, large sections of the Silk Road came under the control of the major civilisations and trade became relatively low-risk. During periods of destabilisation, such as that following the Mongol invasion of the 1300s or the period of British and Russian expansion into the region of the late 1800s, merchants increasingly sought alternative routes and markets.

Trade both promotes an international style and encourages local interpretation and modulations of this. Regional expression of key visual symbols depends in part on the vagaries of understanding and interpretation and the availability of materials and technology. The Buddhist lion, for instance, symbol of the Sakyamuni north Indian clan, found a ready-made symbolic family in the elegant big cats of Scythian, Xiongnu and Mongol arts, and crossed and re-crossed the Silk Road as religious symbol, decorative textile, sculpture and miniature until today it can be found throughout Sydney in its European version as the heraldic lion of New South Wales and in its Chinese version as the paired Buddhist lions of Dixon Street and the Bank of China. This type of imagery continues to play a key role in the arts of Mongolia, Tuva and the Altai, where Buddhism and shamanism are both still practised. In western Central Asia, however, especially in cities such as Bukhara, where Islam, with its prohibition on the making of images of humans and animals, was deeply entrenched, animal imagery is less frequently found, and often the ram, the eagle, the dragon, the phoenix and even the image of the horseman are reduced to abstract terms. A compromise position is found in Kazakh and Turkmen designs, and woven tent bands frequently include animal and human figures.

The rise of the Turkic peoples and the spread of Islam

By the eighth century CE, both the Kazakh steppe and the Silk Road cities from Turfan to Merv were dominated by Turkic people. Though divided into different clans, tribes and hordes, they seem to have a common origin in that group of tribes evicted from the Ordos region by the Xiongnu in 177 BCE, at the beginning of their conflict with Han dynasty China. One major group, the Yuezhi, travelled from the borders of China to the Graeco-Bactrian kingdoms of modern Afghanistan where they established permanent settlements. Others spread throughout Central Asia, gathering strength over the centuries.

When the Parthian empire broke apart during the third century CE, the Turan region between the Caspian and the Aral seas became the home of the nomadic Turkmen who inherited and continued to develop the Tekke horse, which they still regard as the practical and symbolic centre of their culture. By the sixth century CE, allied with other Turkic tribes in Central Asia, they had established the Turkic khaganate. This bloc then formed a coalition with the Sassanian Persians to destroy the empire of the Epthalite Huns, taking over large areas of Bactria, Transoxiana, eastern Iran and modern Pakistan. By the end of the sixth century they had allied with the Byzantines against the Sassanians (softening up this empire for a later Arab conquest) and invaded the Caucasus to establish the Khazar khanate. (A khan is a Central Asian ruler, by birth, election or conquest, having no necessary religious affiliation.)

By this time the Turkic peoples had split into a western khaganate and an eastern bloc with its centre in Mongolia. The eastern group, including the important Uigur tribes, ex-nomads who now controlled the Tarim Basin cities of the Silk Road, became subject to the Tang dynasty Chinese in 630 CE, beginning an enormous resurgence in international trade. By the late seventh century, Turkic khanates could be found from Mongolia to the Black Sea controlling key trade cities such as Bukhara, Samarkand, Kashgar and Khiva, and a rich and flourishing culture characterised by spectacular murals and Buddhist imagery could be found from Nisa to Dunhuang.

In the 600s, the Chinese, under the Tang emperor Taizong (ruled 600–649 CE), re-invaded eastern Central Asia and took control of the trade route through to the Fergana Valley. Throughout this century trade flourished and goods from as far as Byzantium flowed into China. But between 705 and 715 CE the Arabs, who had already conquered much of Iran, launched a holy war into Central Asia, reaching as far as Kashgar before the death of their leader Qutaiba ibn Muslim in 717 CE. Both empires met at the Talas River, where the Arabs defeated the Chinese, driving them back into the Xinjiang region. Although initial Arab attempts to forcibly convert the many Turkic tribes to Islam was met with general revolt, within a few generations most of Central Asia through to the Tarim Basin (controlled by the Chinese with the support of the Uighur tribes) had converted to Islam.

In the late ninth century, as Tang China increasingly lost control of its outermost territories, the Iranian Samanid dynasty took on the administration of Transoxiana, with its capital in Bukhara. New Turkic dynasties were established in Kashgar and Afghanistan, and the Uigurs in the Tarim Basin were finally converted to Islam. The Seljuk Turks moved to the Bukhara region and began an expansion which resulted, by 1055, in the capture of Baghdad. In 1071, under their leader, Arp Arslan (ruled 1063 – 1072), the Seljuks defeated the Byzantine army at Manzikert. They went on to capture Damascus and Jerusalem and, in 1077, established the sultanate of Rum in Anatolia, precipitating the first Crusade in 1097. These invasions were followed by other Turkic groups such as the Ottoman and, by 1453 with the fall of Constantinople (now Istanbul), the old Byzantine empire and much of eastern Europe was under Turkish control.

The Mongol invasions

However, back in the original Turkic homeland in Mongolia, a new power was rising as first the Mongol Khitans moved into Central Asia, to be followed by united Mongol clans under Genghis Khan. The Turkic Kirghiz tribes fled south to the Tien Shan, the Uigurs submitted to Mongol rule and, by 1221, the Mongol conquest of China and Korea, India, the Russian steppes, most of the Arab world and all of Central Asia was complete. The four chief Mongol areas included Yuan dynasty China, Il Khan Iran, Kipchak Russia and the realm of the Golden Horde in the Central Asian steppes.

For a short time there was a flourishing and enormously creative period of trade and exchange of ideas throughout this region. Europeans, such as the Venetian Marco Polo, the French priest Guillaume de Rubruquis and the Roman missionary Giovanni di Montecorvino, travelled through Central Asia as far as the Chinese capital, and reported on its wonders to a disbelieving Europe. Chinese artists and craftspeople moved to Iran and Iraq and brought with them not only aesthetic forms that would influence the development of Persian and Mogul miniatures and textiles, but also knowledge of paper making, gunpowder and clockwork systems, which spread from the Islamic world to Europe within a couple of generations.

Despite this cultural flowering, the period of the Mongol invasions saw the end of the Silk Road as the primary means of international trade. The Mongol Yuan dynasty (1280–1368) coincided with a change in climate, leading to increased desertification in the Tarim Basin. This limited the capacity of many of the eastern Central Asian oasis cities to function as centres of trade, and some rapidly became uninhabitable. At the same time, the violence of the invasions and the slaughter of literally hundreds of thousands of city dwellers led to a breakdown in the essential water supply system. Many cities relied on a network of carefully maintained underground channels and cisterns for both local agriculture and community water. Generally, individual families controlled and took responsibility for different areas of this system. Invaders, rarely understanding the significance of the waterways, frequently destroyed key sections as a means of reducing the walled cities. Moreover, the deaths following the fall of such cities invariably ensured the breakdown of the system of mutually interdependent water responsibilities.

The Shir-dor Madrasah (theological college) in Samerkand, built 1619–1636.

Photo by Frank Cahill, 1995

Also, while trade certainly flourished during the Mongol imperial age, with ever-increasing volumes of goods travelling well-maintained and -policed caravan routes, the Mongols, in keeping with their traditional emphasis on military rather than administrative or mercantile skills, were involved only as protectors and consumers, and never established a merchant class of their own. Their ability to police the caravan routes ceased with fall of the Yuan dynasty in China in 1368, and the succeeding Ming dynasty (1368–1644) lost interest in maintaining control of its Central Asian provinces. Civil wars among the successors of Genghis Khan, division among the Mongol states with the Il Khans and the Kipchaks adopting Islam while Mongolia remained Buddhist, increasing conflict with other Islamic groups and the antagonism to European contact exacerbated by the Crusades all served to bring about a diminishing of the international trade across Central Asia.

The Khanate period and the growth of the 'carpet' cities

In 1336 a second Genghis Khan, Timur (known in Europe as Tamerlane the Great), was born and in 1369 he established the centre of his empire at Samarkand. From his early teens until his death in 1405, he reunited much of Central Asia, and extended his conquests into Russia, India, Iran, Iraq, Afghanistan and Anatolia. In the years following his death, his descendants ruled in Herat and Samarkand, the Black Sheep Turkmen controlled western Iran, the Ottoman Turks finally captured Constantinople, the Uzbeks moved south to Transoxiana and the Kazakh empire was established on the Central Asian steppes. By the early 1700s, when the Mogul empire was established in India, the distribution of people through Central Asia was much as it is today.

Although by this time sea trade had largely usurped the role of the Silk Road, and increasing desertification had marginalised many of the Tarim Basin settlements, major cities of western Central Asia such as Herat, Bukhara, Samarkand, Tashkent, Kokand and Khiva were flourishing as the capital cities of various khanates and emirates (an emir, unlike a khan, claims descent from the Prophet Mohammed and must, of course, be Islamic). As in the second century BCE, cities were the administrative hearts of essentially nomadic tribal groupings, and remained so until well into the 1800s. The principal rulers of many of these khanates were Uzbeks, a relatively new tribal grouping, who formed the military and court elite, while the earlier, sedentary population, the Tajiks, supplied both the agrarian and the financial infrastructure, and the various Turkmen tribes, Yomut, Tekke, Ersari, provided mercenary military support.

Each city became a production centre for Islamic arts—carpets and other textiles; jewellery; metalwork; and spectacular architecture, usually decorated with polychrome tiles as both an aggrandisement of the local ruler and a celebration of Islam. During this time the form of Islam followed by many Central Asian city cultures became narrowly fundamentalist, even fanatical. Any deviation from prescribed beliefs was met with swift and violent punishment, and contact with 'infidels', particularly Christians, was avoided outside the constraints of trade.

Nonetheless, carpets, especially, found a market in the West, and traders and explorers from both eastern and western Europe were drawn to this largely closed world. A fascination with Central Asia and its merchants and military can be found in European writings going back to the 1500s with Christopher Marlowe's *Tamburlaine the Great* (about 1587), and continuing well into the late 1800s with James Elroy Flecker's play, *Hassan* (staged 1923), however, actual contacts were few and usually dangerous. From the 1600s to the late 1800s, Russia and Britain especially began to manipulate the politics of Central Asia. Russia moved first into Siberia, then gradually into Kazakhstan, while Britain inched upward through India. Their presence, both as infidels and as political opportunists, was far from welcome, and 'explorers' and emissaries were often shot at, expelled or murdered.

The 'great game' – Russia and Britain in Central Asia

Throughout the 1800s Britain and Russia continued to expand into Asia, Russia moving down into Central Asia by way of Siberia, the Altai and the Transcaucasus, Britain gradually moving up through India. By the early 1800s, Russia had largely seized control of Kazakhstan, then divided into three weak khanates, and was supporting Turkmen dissent in Bukhara and Khiva. From the 1830s to the 1860s the governor-general of Orenburg in Kazakhstan, Count Vasily Perovsky, pursued a policy of frontier extension and fortification, providing a base for the capture of Tashkent in 1864, and Samarkand and Bukhara in 1868. Khotan and Khiva followed shortly after and, by 1884, with the exception of a small area of the Pamir plateau, the Russian takeover was complete. The building of the Orenburg – Tashkent railway in 1906 linked the region with European Russia.

Although China reconquered Kashgar in 1878, uniting the Tarim Basin territories into the province of Xinjiang, unequal treaties with the Chinese in the second half of the 1800s gave Russia territory on the borders of Xinjiang and Mongolia, and put Chinese control of the region at risk. In 1896, for instance, China gave Russia the right to construct a railway across northern Mongolia, linking with the Trans-Siberian route to Vladivostok and increasing Russian dominance of trade in Central Asia. British interference in China, especially the Opium Wars (1839–1842; 1856–1860) and British control of the Chinese coastal treaty ports such as Guangzhou (Canton) made some accommodation with the Russians seem essential if China were to maintain independence.

Outside coastal China, the British were generally more concerned with consolidating their position in India and ensuring that Russian influence did not extend into northern India or Afghanistan. The British were, in any event, usually blocked by the Afghan rulers with whom they made alliances of varying success. Afghanistan not only maintained its independence, but actually extended its frontiers. The complex mix of strategies, treaties, spying, exploration and exploitation that occurred as the two great powers jockeyed for position came to be known as 'The Great Game'. Some of the players, such as the Russian Colonel Przhevalski and the British adventurers Sir Francis Younghusband and Sir Mark Aurel Stein, combined spying with a genuine interest in documenting Central Asian ethnography, archaeology and geography. Much of our understanding of this fascinating region began with their combination of observation, excavation and often straight-out theft of priceless archaeological and historic treasures such as the Dunhuang library scrolls.

Russian imperial annexation of western Central Asia had only a superficial effect on the lives of the nomads and the oasis city dwellers. Emirs and khans retained their thrones as vassals of Russia; Islam remained the principal religion; and, though Russian peasants moved into some areas of Kazakhstan, life for most people went on as before. Urban-based reform movements, both in Russian Central Asia and Afghanistan, met with strong opposition from conservative Islamic clergy and little support from local Russian administrators. However, the period following World War I, after the Bolshevik Revolution in Russia, revived British interest in the Great Game and briefly encouraged independence and reform movements in the Central Asian states.

Communism and beyond

By the 1920s, most of the former khanates had overthrown their rulers and established autonomous people's republics. Over the next decade, with varying degrees of violence, Kazakhstan, Uzbekistan, Turkmenistan, Tajikistan and Kyrgyzstan were incorporated into the Soviet Union and boundaries similar to today's were established along ethnic lines, involving considerable population movement. Rebellions, such as that in Turkmenistan in the 1930s, were harshly put down and thousands of Turkmen, Uzbek and Kazakh communists, including the president and the premier of Turkmenistan, were executed. Stalin's policy of forced collectivisation, begun in the 1920s, was a disaster, especially for Kazakhstan, where over 2 750 000 people died either from famine or reprisals between 1925 and 1933. Attempts at turning nomadic pastoralists into settled agriculturalists failed as a social experiment, and, more significantly, made inappropriate use of land. In Uzbekistan, where cotton became a major crop, taking up lands previously dedicated to grazing and small-scale intensive farming, the resulting environmental disaster is yet to be contained.

At the same time, revolts in Xinjiang left the area subject to the control of a variety of Chinese- and Soviet-backed warlords until the Chinese communists re-established control of the region in the 1940s, resulting in a mass exodus of Kazakhs to Soviet Central Asia. The period of World War II and its immediate aftermath also saw the forced migration of minority ethnic groups from many regions of the Soviet Union into Central Asia—Chechens, Tartars, Georgian Turks, Koreans, Germans, Ukranians and Russians among them. By the 1950s, the Kazakhs, for instance, made up just under 30 per cent of the Kazakhstan population. This, combined with collectivisation and the enforcement of Soviet values including a strongly anti-Islamic sentiment, combined to devalue the traditions and traditional lifestyles of both nomadic and urban Central Asians.

However, the recent break-up of the Soviet Union and the re-emergence of the smaller nations of Central Asia, Siberia and the Caucasus have encouraged a reassessment of the values

of tradition and a passionate inquiry into the history of the various regions.

The break-up of the Soviet Union has not been without incident, especially in the Caucasus where ethnic groups such as the Armenians and the Azerbaijanis are struggling to re-establish boundaries, and other peoples such as the Chechen are still not free of Russian control. There has also been a major exodus of ethnic Russians from senior administrative and educative positions in most of former Soviet Central Asia, and it has sometimes been difficult to re-establish and maintain the services they ran. Fortunately, the major potential for internal conflict, the kind of ethnic cleansing that has characterised the break-up of former Yugoslavia, has so far been unrealised—with the exception of the disastrous civil war in Tajikistan.

But autonomy has not been restored to Chinese Central Asia and the policy of Han Chinese settlement in Mongolia, Tibet and Xinjiang (ethnic Chinese now make up some 38 per cent of Xinjiang's population) has led to a more explosive situation. Human rights abuses are rife in all three regions; religious freedom is severely restricted (whether of Tibetan Buddhists or Turkic Muslims); peaceful demonstrations are met with violence; and the detention and even death of political activists is commonplace. Amnesty International reports that in 1990, for instance, as many as 50 people were killed during a demonstration near Kashgar, while hundreds, possibly thousands, were imprisoned.

Xinjiang, like much of Central Asia, is oil-rich, and control of this region is essential to China's economy. In former Soviet Central Asia, the Eurasian hinterland is once again central to a 'great game' of politics, economics and cultural influence. This time the major prize is control of the enormously rich oil reserves under the Caspian Sea and in the republics of Kazakhstan, Turkmenistan and Uzbekistan, and the major players are the United States and Russia.

The long conflict in Afghanistan between US-supported conservative tribal people and the Russian-supported urban government resulted in the resurgence of fundamentalist Islam, an end which suited neither great power. Both fear a similar outcome in former Soviet Central Asia.

Oil has become the new silk, and the need for a pipeline to carry the Central Asian riches westward is a dominant theme in the new politics. The US-based Chevron Corporation has developed the giant Tengiz oil field in Kazakhstan but pipelines need to cross disputed territory, especially in the Caucasus. At present, oil brought in tankers via Istanbul is causing shipping problems in the Bosporus Straits, and there have been accidents involving burning vessels. A pipeline through to Turkey would provide a safer and cheaper route, but the Central Asian republics may prefer to deal with Iran or with their former Russian colleagues.

The United States needs to sustain the economic and social independence of the new nations, and so gain access to essential oil reserves and export routes. This requires the difficult balancing act of encouraging the emergence of secular yet Muslim societies, which reject both Russian economic dominance of the region and the militant, anti-Western Islamic fundamentalism of countries such as Afghanistan, Pakistan and Iran. Russia, on the other hand, needs to control distribution through the potential pipeline routes, and is best served at present by perpetuating ethnic and other conflicts in the Caucasus region (Abkhazia, Armenia, Azerbaijan, Chechnya, Dagestan, Georgia) while continuing to maintain good relations with the oil-producing nations.

The new nations of Kazakhstan, Kyrgyzstan, Tadikistan, Turkmenistan and Uzbekistan, together with the Altai and Tuva, seem increasingly eager to encourage both international investment and international tourism. All have made surprisingly rapid and effective use of the Internet as a resource, marketing themselves in both English and Russian. At the same time, there has been a marked emphasis on traditional culture and values, long suppressed by the communists, creating a resurgence of interest in traditional crafts and skills, as well as in Islamic saints and regional heroes. Sometimes this has lead to fairly extreme positions, as when the Altaic Republic refused to permit further excavation of Saka-Scythian grave sites (sites of enormous archaeological interest to Russian and other academics), on the grounds that this is disturbing to their buried ancestors. Similarly, Xinjiang Muslims objected to images of mosques being displayed at the recent exhibition on Chinese Central Asia in Florida on the grounds that they were presented as tourist sites of architectural interest rather than holy places. Inner Mongolians have also actively resented the promotion of their traditional way of life as a tourism gimmick by the Chinese government.

Such reactions are balanced by a newly emergent sense of identity and self-confidence. And, perhaps, the establishment of the Karakoram Highway, the upgrading of regional airports and the positive self-marketing of these nations may foreshadow a new 'Silk Road' age when goods, ideas, technologies and art flow freely again from east to west and back.

Entertainers from one of the oasis towns in Uzbekistan in the late 1800s, dressed in ikat-patterned khalats *(coats).*

Photo from *Traditional Textiles of Central Asia* by Janet Harvey, 1996.
Photographer anon

Nomads & oasis dwellers: the people and their textiles

Christina Sumner

The people who inhabit the great sweeping curves of desert and oasis, mountain and steppe that make up Central Asia, and that stretch from the Caspian Sea to Siberia, are generally characterised as having traditionally followed either a nomadic (pastoral) or a settled (agrarian) way of life. This division into two modes of economic subsistence was fostered by the geography. In the north are great arid steppelands, best suited to seasonal grazing, and in the south a fertile arc conducive to agriculture and settlement.

In reality, the history of the peoples of Central Asia is very much more complex and bloody than this simplistic and harmonious-sounding duality of nomadic/settled makes it seem. The history can be more realistically understood as an epic tale of interaction and merging, marauding, raiding and trading as, over time, the people practising these two ways of living came into contact and very often conflict, nomadic tribe against village and town, tribe against tribe, city against city. Fortunes waxed and waned, nomadic people settled and grew crops, farmers took to the hills with flocks of animals, empires rose and fell, people interbred and a great blending occurred.

Although the distinction between the nomadic and settled people of Central Asia and their ways of life is blurred, it nevertheless serves as a useful framework in any consideration of the material culture of the region. Both nomadic and urban groups produced beautiful textiles, and other goods, with which they dressed and ornamented themselves, and their very different domestic and ritual environments. Traditional Central Asian textiles in particular tend to take characteristic nomadic or urban forms, although their use was not restricted to their own cultural arena and exchanges were the norm; town-made coats, for example, were worn by nomadic people and nomadic rugs were laid on urban floors.

A symbiotic relationship

Nomads are pastoralists. They are economically dependent on their herds of animals and move seasonally from pasture to pasture in order to find good grazing for them. Because they are so often on the move and because of their dependence on animals, the material culture of the nomadic people of Central Asia is characterised by portability and by the use of raw materials derived from their animals. For herding, Central Asian nomads chose sheep and goats, which provided both food and wool. For transport, they relied primarily on horses and camels, and it was these, both for riding and as pack animals, that made their seasonal migrations possible. Consequently, horses in particular and camels were very highly prized. It has been said that Turkmen love their horses more than their wives and children, and are more concerned for their horses' welfare than their own.

For nomadism to be successful, that is, to ensure economic survival and human wellbeing for the group, the migratory routes to good grazing land must be open and an adequate water supply available. Nomads must also be prosperous enough to own the necessary tents, coverings, carrying bags, animal trappings, weapons and tools. Wealth, when not tied up in the nomads' animals, often traditionally took the form of wonderful jewellery. Different nomadic groups or tribes used their own particular range of abstract patterns and motifs to decorate their textiles and trappings. These distinctive patterns were memorised by the women and passed down from one generation to the next. The patterns are a primary means of identifying the source of a particular rug or felt or embroidery. It has been estimated that each nomadic family unit needed about 100 kilograms of wool a year to make their own clothing and felts, which is roughly equivalent to a hundred large, thick woollen sweaters.

Settled people, on the other hand, practise agriculture, laying claim to tracts of arable land; fencing their fields; sowing crops; and building villages, towns and cities, armies and bureaucracies. Around the oasis towns of western Central Asia, the farming of cotton and mulberries (mulberry leaves are fed to silkworms) was of major economic importance and these crops took up a large proportion of cultivable land. Because they had permanent homes, the city-dwelling agriculturalists of Central Asia were not constrained by size or weight or a limited range of raw materials in their creativity, which has notably produced fine textiles of silk and cotton, goldwork embroidery, decorative metalwork, ceramics and woodwork – as well as great and monumental architecture.

The clothing and domestic textiles made in the urban centres of Central Asia were quite different in form from those made by nomadic groups. While nomads produced carpets, tents, tent furnishings and animal trappings, mostly in rich dark reds, blues and browns, settled people produced large wall hangings and fine silks, which tended to be more delicate and lighter in weight and colour. However, in much the same way as the motifs used in nomadic weavings were indicative of the maker's tribal membership, in towns and cities the patterns of the silk outer robes worn by men served as a sign of the wearer's place in the urban hierarchy.

It has always been in the best interests of pastoralists and agriculturalists to trade their goods with one another; to exchange animal products such as meat, milk, wool and leather for agricultural products such as grain, fruit, silk and cotton, as well as for crafts from urban workshops. However, some nomadic groups, particularly the Turkmen, could not resist helping themselves to the riches of the oasis towns. Raiding, slaughtering and pillaging were part of the tribal way of life; they did not consider it a virtue to die peacefully in bed. The urban dwellers responded to such incursions with organised military action. Consequently, relationships between nomads and townspeople fluctuated considerably. This repeating pattern of trading and raiding was complicated over time by the fact that so many townships and settled communities were established or were partially populated by nomadic peoples when they were forced to abandon pastoralism for economic reasons.

Turkic peoples and their nomadic inheritance

Nomadism evolved in prehistoric times as the indigenous Indo-Europeans of Central Asia moved gradually westwards, and left behind them a vacuum. This vacuum was filled by waves of warring tribespeople from different cultural and linguistic groups who gradually moved westwards from the steppelands north of China in search of new pastures. The aggressive nature of pastoral nomadism arises from competition for the best grazing land, which is of course neither formally owned nor fenced. The incoming peoples spoke a range of related Turkic languages, shared the subsistence economy of pastoral nomadism, and are the ancestors of the Turkmen, Uzbek, Kazakh and Kyrgyz people of Central Asia, for whom the present-day independent states of Turkmenistan, Uzbekistan, Kazakhstan and Kyrgyzstan are named. The fifth state, Tajikistan, is named for the Tajiks, who speak a Persian language and, as descendants of the original Indo-European population, represent the earliest settled people of the area.

Twenty-four different Turkmen tribes were listed by the Persian historian Rashid al-Din (1247–1318); today Turkmen people live in north-eastern Iran and northern Afghanistan as well as Turkmenistan. Turkmen women are noted for their superbly woven carpets, rugs, and the bags and trappings of tent-dwelling nomadic life. Of these, the Salor Turkmen are generally considered the finest weavers, while others noted for their textile artistry are the Tekke, who were the dominant Turkmen tribe during the 1800s, and the Ersari, Yomut, Saruk and Chodor people.

The origins of Turkmen rug weaving are hard to determine, as no examples made earlier than about 1800 survive. The most characteristic feature of Turkmen design is the *gul*, a rather angular, often octagonal, motif that is repeated across the field of a Turkmen rug or bag face. Each tribe has its own typical *guls*, major and minor (large and small), which enable us to recognise the particular tribal source of most weavings. The source of these motifs may be the ubiquitous Chinese and Sassanian silks, carried as common trade goods along the Silk Road through Central Asia. The Turkmen were presumably exposed to these silks, which were patterned with roundels containing flowers and animals, and with smaller lozenge-shaped motifs, both of which may have been abstracted by the Turkmen to suit carpet-weaving technology and to form the *guls*. From the 1500s, Timurid miniatures portray rugs with similar roundels, used as repeating motifs, and with calligraphic borders that also have strong links to later Turkmen designs. It is perhaps the nomadic nature of Turkmen society, whose women customarily wove patterns from memory, that has encouraged the use of smaller repeating motifs rather than the large complex medallions and interlaced patterns featured in city workshop carpets.

Prior to the arrival of the Russians in what was then known as Turkestan in the mid to late 1800s, the Turkmen relied on raiding and slave trading for their livelihood. When these activities were outlawed, they had to resort to formal trading and their carpets, produced by women from surplus wool, emerged as economically significant commodities in the marketplace. Over the centuries, the Turkmen blended with the sedentary population of Turkmenistan and, by the 1800s, many lived in rammed-earth houses and were also skilled in agriculture.

The Uzbeks, who share a nomadic heritage with the Turkmen and also speak a Turkic language, were originally a mixed group of unrelated tribal people. They are said to have taken their name from Uzbek Khan (who ruled from 1313 to 1341), a descendant of Genghis Khan (1162–1227), who had banded them together under his leadership. When Uzbek Khan was converted to Islam he pursuaded his Uzbek subjects to follow suit.

A special cover called a kejebe *conceals a Yomut Turkmen bride riding to her new home. The camel is decorated befitting the occasion. The photo was taken in 1967, north of the city of Gombad-e Kavus in Iran.*

Photo by William Irons, courtesy William Irons

Today's Uzbeks are descended from a blending of ancient tribal groups with the original Iranian population of the area. Some Uzbeks adopted the Tajiks' urban culture; others, such as the fiercely independent Lakai Uzbek, lived a nomadic life; while others were semi-nomadic, lived on the outskirts of urban settlements and practised agriculture. The Uzbek tribal repertoire includes pile and flat-weave rugs, felted rugs, and embroidered bags, purses, belts, tent ornaments and animal trappings. Settled Uzbeks farmed silk and cotton, and produced some of the world's most strikingly patterned silks (made by men in workshops) and embroideries (made by women in domestic environments). Uzbek textiles were thus produced in a variety of cultural contexts and the exceptional variety of pattern found in them is the result of disparate historical and cultural influences.

Islam, the religion to which the Uzbeks adhered, was a major influence on Central Asian carpet and textile design. The concept that Allah is everywhere is reflected in the potential for infinite repetition seen in Islamic pattern in, for example, architectural ornament, and the fields and borders of rugs. Islamic artists were prohibited from representing living beings, in case people regarded them as objects of worship; strict Muslim theologians also held that Allah was the only one who could create life. Where people and animals were represented, they were often highly abstracted. Designers generally favoured floral motifs and developed a scrollwork design with winding leafy stems, known as arabesque. These practices, together with the geometric interpretations of pre-Islamic patterns and motifs, such as stylised ram's heads, suns, birds and animals, have ensured that the patterns are highly decorative.

Kazakh women weaving a tent band on a horizontal ground loom in the 1890s.

The Kazakhs, who inhabit the northern steppes of Central Asia, speak a Turkic language and are the largest group of nomads who still choose to live in felt tents, despite decades of efforts to house them in settlements, re-educate them and convert them to cooperative farming by Russian authorities. By the mid 1800s, most Kazakhs were firmly under Russian rule. Russian farmers had moved into the fertile northern steppes and fields of grain were planted on the Kazakhs' traditional campsites, which cut their migratory routes. At the same time, Uzbeks and Tajiks were extending their cultivated lands in the south of the Kazakh's traditional lands. With the imposition of Russian administrative systems and taxes, and the loss of rich pasturage, many Kazakhs abandoned pastoralism fully or in part and took up farming or other diverse forms of employment. As a result of these external influences, the traditional socio-cultural structures of the Kazakhs were disrupted and weakened, and they became more and more dependent on trade goods, including textiles from Russia and Turkestan. A preference emerged for factory-made flower prints and Russian-style velvet jackets.

The Kyrgyz are an ethnic group who also speak a Turkic language, and many of them still follow a nomadic way of life in eastern Central Asia. While many of the Kyrgyz maintained their nomadic lifestyle under Tsarist Russia, there was an increase in agriculture, trade and mining. The traditional textiles produced by the Kyrgyz are very similar to those of the Kazakhs, and included reed screens, rugs, trappings, and wonderful felts and embroideries. Perhaps the best known of these are their *chii* (wool-wrapped reed screens) and the brilliant felts, whose designs resemble those on objects found in the Pazyryk (fifth century BCE) and Noin Ula tombs (first century BCE). Both the Kyrgyz and the Kazakhs make mosaic felts in which either coloured wools are laid out in patterns and felted together or already-felted coloured cloths are cut into corresponding patterns and fitted together like a jigsaw puzzle, with white outlining cord concealing the joins. The Kyrgyz also wear moulded felt hats.

All four of these groups—Turkmen, Uzbeks, Kazakhs and Kyrgyz—have thus, in addition to their strong nomadic traditions, at different times and to different degrees, embraced settled living.

Further complicating the ethnic mix of Mongols, Turks and Indo-Europeans was the influx of Arabs into Central Asia from the south from the eighth century onwards. Having observed the lack of centralised political power resulting from the feudal nature of Central Asian society, the Arabs were quick to move into the area, bringing their religion of Islam with them. They learned to speak the language of the region where they settled, associated themselves with the local elites, and generally merged with the local culture. Islam became the dominant religion of the entire area as far east as the Altai Mountains and has had a profound effect on social and cultural life. Architecture and decorative art became the focus of creative activity and calligraphy was added as ornament to the existing geometric, abstract and floral motifs. Inscriptions in Arabic with a religious or moral content were intended to promote Islam through their sheer beauty, while geometric patterns were given a theoretical base in the rapid development of mathematics and applied geometry between the tenth and twelfth centuries.

Over the last century or so, many Arabs have moved south into northern Afghanistan, while a large proportion of the present day population of Uzbekistan is of Arab origin. Arab weavers produce large flat-weave rugs for sale for urban buildings, and a variety of mostly flat-weave rugs and bags for their own use.

Another significant ethnic group are the Baluchi, who are also principally tent-dwelling nomads and produce a distinctive range of textiles. The Baluchi speak a language related to Persian and probably migrated from Iran, where many still live, into southern Central Asia, Afghanistan and western Pakistan. There are also some Baluchi around Merv in Turkmenistan. Baluchi flat-weave and pile rugs and trappings show great subtlety in their fine patterns and are often ornamented with shells from the Arabian sea, and bone and glass beads.

Yurts, women and textile production

Central Asian nomadic people inhabit a very harsh landscape and have learned to take care of their basic needs extraordinarily well, constructing for themselves remarkably colourful and luxurious domestic environments. They live traditionally in domed circular felt tents, called yurts, whose domes reflect those of the city mosques. A yurt is internally divided into areas for cooking and living; the living area may, in turn, be divided between men and women. In Islamic society, to which Central Asian nomads belong, the home is regarded as a sanctified space and merits respect.

A Tekke Turkmen woman standing on a khali *(main tent carpet) in front of the yurt in the early 1900s. She is wearing her jewellery, and an ikat-patterned robe made in one of the oasis towns of Uzbekistan.*

Photo by Sergei Mikhailovich Prokudin-Gorski

Central Asian yurts are collapsible and transportable, and typically have a latticework structure covered with felts and secured by decorative woven tent bands. For weddings and other special occasions, specially wide and very beautiful bands are brought out and wound around the yurt. The owners take enormous pride in the appearance and furnishing of these moveable homes. The considerable creativity and artistry lavished on them are particularly evident in the tent bands, rugs, cushions, and a range of storage bags of different shapes and sizes that serve both practical and highly decorative functions.

The yurt and its contents can be set up and dismantled by women within two or three hours. It can be transported on two camels, with another camel to carry the furnishings. The very high value placed by nomads (particularly men) on their camels and horses is reflected in the wonderful array of woven and embroidered decorative trappings used to ornament the animals – shaped blankets and saddle covers, flank trappings, head and rump harnesses, knee pads and, for Turkmen horses, special silver and carnelian-studded leather horse jewellery.

The production of textiles in Central Asian nomadic societies is traditionally the province of women, although the shearing is done by men and it is the men who take any surplus goods to market. Spinning, weaving and felt making are done in and around the yurt while the women also manage child care. These tasks are a woman's primary and very important economic contribution to her family. Young girls learn the skills of textile production from an early age, under the supervision of an older woman, and the designs used by their particular tribal group are committed to memory over many years of training and practice. By their early twenties, most young Turkmen women are skilled weavers and those who have not yet had children may expect to spend up to 12 hours a day weaving. In addition to making textiles for their family's own needs, nomadic women produce rugs for town and village people, many of whom were once nomadic themselves and want nomadic rugs for their permanent homes.

The women of most nomadic groups also produce superb embroideries. These include the densely embroidered *chyrpys* (silk coats) with long false sleeves worked by Tekke Turkmen women until the early 1900s. These had different coloured ground cloth depending on the age and marital status of the woman wearing them and were worn for special festivals. They are still made, but without the false sleeves and with less embroidery. Also notable is the wide range of striking geometric and curvilinear bags for storage and transport produced by different nomadic Uzbek peoples, who have developed purely decorative versions of these (often without backs) for urban markets. In northern Afghanistan and Pakistan, Hazar and Pushtun women create elaborate embroidered decoration on clothing and small bags, purses and accessories.

The oasis towns

The urban centres of Central Asia were established at the many green oases watered by rivers from the surrounding mountains. With the growth of overland trade routes along the Silk Road during the first millenium BCE, trading centres grew up at regular intervals. Water, food and shelter were available at these caravan towns and goods, which changed hands many times along the route, were bought and sold. The fortunes of these towns and their associated agricultural areas fluctuated greatly, as their survival was dependent on a number of factors, including access to water. Increasing desertification has taken its toll, and when irrigation systems were disabled by the shortsighted action of marauding nomadic groups, the settlements often could not survive.

The urban centres were for centuries organised politically as city-states or khanates, each ruled by a local khan (chieftain or governor). The names of these great cities—Herat and Bukhara, Samarkand, Khiva and Merv—conjure romantic images of fabled wealth and splendour. They also call to mind the remarkable artistic and architectural legacy of the Mongol ruler Timur (also known as Tamerlane) (1336–1405), whose strong adherence to Islam ensured the widespread establishment of the Islamic religion and Islamic art and culture in Central Asia. Some of the largest and most impressive mosques and monuments in the Islamic world, with their great domes and brilliantly coloured and patterned tile surfaces, can be found in Central Asia.

Under Timur and his successors, Central Asia became a major cultural centre. Skilled artisans were forceably settled in Samarkand, Timur's capital, and other Central Asian cities. Their great skills enabled local ruling families to establish enormous wealth through the magnificent textiles, books, ceramics, jewellery and metalwork these artisans produced. The influence of the Timurid period, and of Islam, to which the vast majority of Central Asian population were converted, pervades all forms of Central Asian art and is evident in the repeat patterns and floral imagery of Central Asian textiles. Of all the textile art produced in the urban centres of Central Asia, the best known are the brilliantly patterned and coloured silk, or silk and cotton, ikat-dyed robes and panels, and the large silk on cotton embroidered hangings known collectively as *suzanis*.

Textiles for urban living

Silk and cotton production has long been a primary focus for the settled agriculturalists of the oases. During the 1800s, having colonised Turkestan, Russia promoted the cultivation of cotton and mulberry trees and, until the Soviet regime was established in the 1920s, the production of silk and cotton fabrics was run as a cottage industry with a clear division of labour. Women were responsible for the rearing of the silkworms and they wove the cotton fabrics that were widely distributed for both home use and export, while men were responsible for producing silk fabrics. Cotton and silk crops, which are economically very important to the region, now account for half the irrigated land in Uzbekistan, but the fertilisers and pesticides needed to support them have seriously affected both the land and the health of the population.

A merchant and his wares — printed and woven cottons made in Tsarist Russia — in one of the oasis towns in the early 1900s.

Photo by Sergei Mikhailovich Prokudin-Gorski

29

A man weaving a length of ikat-patterned cloth near Margellan in eastern Uzbekistan, mid 1990s.

Photo by John Gillow, mid 1990s

A range of cotton fabrics were produced by the urban Uzbeks during the 1800s. One of the principal cotton products was a brightly coloured striped cloth called *alacha*, which was produced in large quantities in Samarkand and other centres until about 1960. *Alacha* was the main material used to make both summer and winter coats, or *khalats*. Other primary cotton products were *baz* (plain) and *chit* (block-printed) cottons. By the end of the 1800s, these had been superseded in the market place by factory-printed cottons from Iran and Russia. It is these printed fabrics, which are often in shades of red with white, yellow and black accents, that we see as linings in the ikat and embroidered coats, bags and trappings of both urban and nomadic people.

A number of different silk fabrics were woven in Central Asia, but the best known are the wonderful bright ikat silks or *abr* (meaning cloud) which were used to make *pardah* (wall hangings), and men's and women's clothing, and can be found in a variety of other textile goods. Production of these tie-dyed silks and silk-cotton blends flourished in the cities of present day Uzbekistan, particularly in Bukhara but also in Samarkand and Fergana at least as early as the 1700s. Research suggests that the ikat technique, known locally as *abrbandi*, of tie-dyeing warp threads prior to weaving came to Central Asia from India, or possibly southern China, around the seventh century. There are two main types of ikat in Central Asia: firstly, full ikat, where the entire warp is tie-dyed and the order of the threads is set at the time of dyeing; secondly, strip ikat, in which long skeins are tie-dyed and the pattern is determined by the way these strips are positioned on the loom, often alternating with plain warps.

By the late 1800s, factory-produced silks were already threatening the production of ikats within family groups. Under Soviet rule the general view was that traditional methods were not economically viable, and consequently they were discouraged. Production continues, however, in the Fergana valley, often using garish synthetic dyestuffs and, now that women are permitted to leave the domestic sphere and go to work, with women rather than men at the looms.

Ikat-patterned *khalats* were worn by both men and women, mostly for ceremonial and ritual use. In the urban centres, a man's position in the social, governmental and economic scheme of things was extremely important and his dress reflected his rank in society. The cut of these brightly coloured robes varied very little but the materials they were made of, the structure of the fabric and the manner of ornamentation were all indicative of the wearer's status. The lowest ranks wore robes of *adras* (silk and cotton), while the highest wore silk velvet ikat – sometimes embellished with goldwork embroidery. At least until the late 1800s under the despotic khans, it was a punishable offence to wear a robe you were not entitled to wear.

Women's ikat coats were cut in much the same way as the men's and were worn over a dress (or dresses) and trousers, although women's coats can often be distinguished from men's by their more open breastline. Many women's coats also had gathers decorated with needlepoint under the sleeve; the gathers gave a fuller skirt and flattered the figure. While young women's dresses had horizontal necklines, those of married women had a deep slit to facilitate breast feeding; originally, both types of dress were cut wide and straight, and had very long sleeves that covered the hands. Today, Uzbek women still wear brilliantly coloured ikat dresses over ikat trousers, but the body is set into a yoke, the sleeves are usually short, the fabrics are often synthetic and, on some of them, the ikat pattern is printed. As earlier, the differences between these garments lie in the great variety of pattern and design rather than in the cut.

The designs used to pattern ikats were mainly inspired by flowers, fruit and animals. They varied greatly and new ones appeared regularly according to the dictates of local fashion. Early ikat designs are often extraordinarily fine and complex, and use up to seven colours but, by the late 1800s, bold and brilliantly coloured geometric figures were the norm. These were often produced through greatly enlarging an earlier pattern. Under pressure from the competition supplied by Russian factory products, ikat producers gradually opted for simpler patterns that could be completed more quickly without loss of quality.

A group of women wearing ikat-patterned dresses in Samarkand in 1995. They are rehearsing for a performance that will mark the visit of a foreign dignitary.

Photo by Frank Cahill, 1995

The large and very beautiful flower-strewn embroideries known as *suzanis* (from the Persian word for needle) were made in and around Bukhara, Shakhrisabz, Nurata, Samarkand, Tashkent and Pskent, in what is now Uzbekistan, and were used as wall hangings, bed covers and room dividers. In public spaces, such as inns, *suzanis* were used to mark the women's quarters and were hung over the doorways that led to these segregated rooms. *Suzanis* were designed to hang in houses not yurts and are, like ikat silks, characteristic of urban textile production; however, whereas ikat silks were produced by men, *suzanis* were made exclusively by women.

Suzanis were an important component of a girl's dowry, and work on the dowry *suzanis* would begin soon after the birth of a daughter. They were made in a range of sizes for specific purposes, the larger ones for wall hangings and room dividers, and the smaller pieces to cover bridal cushions, tables and rolled-up bedding during the day. One form of *suzani*, called a *ruidjo*, was embroidered along the two long sides and one short side only, and was used as a spread for the bridal bed. Large *suzanis* were made by several women in the family. Strips of locally woven cotton cloth were loosely stitched together lengthways to form the size of *suzani* required and a senior woman or *kalamkash* (professional designer) would draw the design on the cloth; the strips were then separated for embroidering with loosely spun silk yarns. Once they were finished, the strips were sewn together again to make the whole.

Suzani designs varied from region to region. Those from Bukhara, Samarkand, Shakhrisabz and Nurata consist mostly of flowers and leaves, sometimes derived from the ancient tree of life form. Floral patterns allude to growth and fertility and, although they reflect the Islamic prohibition on figurative representation, they also appealed to oasis dwellers who were surrounded by desert. The strong circular motifs on *suzanis* from Tashkent and Pskent are more reminiscent of suns and stars than flowers, and are perhaps derived from pre-Islamic cosmological symbols. Occasionally a tiny fish, bird or water jug is embroidered among the flowers on a *suzani*, and sometimes triangular motifs with comb-like projections (often referred to as the female amulet) or scattered flame-shaped motifs, which reflect the Central Asian belief in the protective forces of fire and light, appear. The colours of the embroidery silks vary from place to place, as do the stitches, although the most often encountered are ordinary and closely worked open chain stitch for outlining and, as a filling stitch, a form of couching, called *basma*, which has a number of variants that produce different textural effects.

Internal and external influences

The distinct differences between the carpets, trappings, textiles and clothing produced by nomadic people and settled people can be understood primarily as responses to the practical and cultural requirements and constraints of either a mobile or sedentary lifestyle, and the available materials. In addition to the influence that lifestyle brought to bear on the material culture of the two groups, recognition must also be given to the impact on form and design of the richly varied ethnic mix of Central Asia's population and to its geographical location. With the major cultural centres of Iran, Greece and Rome to the west, Russia to the north, China and Mongolia to the east and India to the south, the people of Central Asia were subject to considerable and persuasive outside influences over a long period of time.

Many of these influences, in the form of materials, technologies, patterns and ideologies, moved into and through Central Asia, east to west and north to south, via the legendary Silk Road, or roads, that connected the Mediterranean world with China and Japan. This effective trading network of interacting nomadic and settled groups was already in operation over 2000 years ago. The routes converged as they crossed Central Asia, and along them travelled silk, horses and a profusion of luxury goods. At different times, depending on availability and consumer demand, the camel caravans carried gold and silver, ceramics and glass, woollens, fur, lacquerware and mirrors, wine, spices and medicinal plants, and other exotica. Stylistic influences and ideologies were also transmitted along the trade route, and were absorbed by the local cultures. The passage of Buddhist monks through Central Asia from the second century CE and the coming of Islam in the ninth were particularly strong influences, and gave rise to a wealth of magnificently ornamented monasteries and mosques. Islam in particular has strongly influenced the textile designs of both urban and nomadic people.

The majority of traders travelled a section of the road only, so that goods were moved from trader to trader and from one oasis town to the next. These trading centres—Bukhara, Balkh, Samarkand, Merv, Kashgar, Khiva and Fergana—also served as entrepots for the exchange of imported goods for locally made products, such as the richly coloured rugs brought in by the nomads.

The strongest and most transformative influence on the material culture of western Central Asia during the 1800s and early 1900s was that of Tsarist Russia, whose pressing need for more agricultural land and new markets for its industrial products brought soldiers and officials into the region. Following expansionist forays southwards into the Caucasus and the steppes of Kazakhstan in the early 1800s, Russia shifted its imperialist sights to the oases of Turkestan and, one by one, the khanates came under Russian rule, thus bringing Russian armies ever closer to the borders of British India. By 1900, the Russian and British empires were separated only by the narrow strip of north-eastern Afghanistan.

Under Tsarist and Soviet rule

The social and economic policies of, firstly, Tsarist and then Soviet and Chinese governments during the 1800s and 1900s radically altered traditional ways of life in Central Asia, although Islamic legal, administrative and educational systems were retained. Because political independence was construed as a threat to the neighbouring sedentary states, many nomadic groups were forced to abandon their migratory lifestyle and settle in the villages and towns. The production of nomadic rugs and trappings consequently declined.

The primary economic reason for the Russian advance into Turkestan was to secure the exchange of locally grown cotton for Russian manufactured goods. American cotton plants were introduced into the oasis plantations in the late 1800s, and more and more land was turned over to cotton cultivation to meet the demands of Russian textile manufacturers. Traditional peasant landholders suffered and merchants profited, while competition from Russian goods weakened the local craft production, on which many oasis dwellers depended for a living. Producers in both workshops and domestic environments cared less for quality when their goods were intended the Russian markets. Islam grew in strength, education improved, and a Muslim intelligentsia developed within the new middle class.

Industrialisation in Russia required a supply of cotton from Central Asia and, in return, released flood of cheap fabrics onto local markets; the local production of ikats and other handwoven fabrics decreased. In the mid 1800s, the invention of synthetic dyes rapidly changed the palette of Central Asian weavers and embroiderers, and their colourful textiles acquired a harsher and less predictable quality.

In 1920, following the Bolshevik Revolution, the Soviet Union took control in western Central Asia; Soviet rule lasted for 70 years. The Turkestan economy had collapsed following the revolution, and efforts were made to re-establish the production of cotton, silk and wool, which were all in demand as raw materials to revive the Soviet economy. Russians congregated in the oasis cities, bringing about changes in education, language and the production of material goods. Craft guilds were converted to unions and small workshops were combined to form cooperatives under one roof in the process of their transformation into factories. Although local people preferred traditional decorations for their homes and the Soviet government encouraged the instruction of young people by master artisans, the impact of industrialisation and Russian imports has been overwhelmingly deleterious to traditional craft forms.

During the 20th century, the efforts of Soviet administrators to direct traditional craft workers away from individual practice and into mass production in Soviet factories led to a further reduction of traditional output. Fortunately, Soviet artists, writers and scholars have also observed and documented many aspects of Central Asian art and culture, providing us with most of what we know today of Central Asian textiles and textile production during the 1800s and 1900s.

Despite multinational immigration, collectivisation and settlement programs, nomadism survives on the Kazakh steppes, in large part due to the Soviet Union's need for the products of pastoralism—wool, hides, meat and dairy products. Sheep, horses and cattle have flourished, although the number of camels has dropped. Yurt living also survives, and yurts are often erected as preferred summer residences alongside more permanent homes, with a range of embroidered yurt decorations that often reflect the floral influence of Uzbek or Russian folk art rather than traditional patterns. Kazakh women continue to make felts with traditional motifs, though in new colours with the introduction of aniline dyes, and Kyrgyz women make flat-weave rugs, often working together on a large piece.

Most of the nomadic and urban rugs and textiles we see today in museums, galleries and private collections were produced against the Russia-dominated political backdrop of the 1800s and early 1900s. Those were turbulent times, marked by oppression and suppression, colonial ambition, world wars and cold wars, border skirmishes, collectivisation and, eventually, glasnost and perestroika. In the summer of 1991, following the break-up of the Soviet Union, the republics of Kazakhstan, Kyrgystan, Tajikistan, Turkmenistan and Uzbekistan declared their independence.

The general decline in the production of traditional crafts during this time was interrupted from time to time by revivals, prompted by periods when imported fabrics were scarce or when there was a change in Soviet attitudes. During the period following World War II, when food was in short supply, Russian factories produced carpets that imitated Turkmen designs to exchange for foodstuffs. In the 1960s, Soviet interest in traditional crafts began to grow and there was a revival in ikat production. Consequently, some of the traditional skills still survive. Their importance is widely appreciated in the newly independent states where they are proudly acknowledged as valued continuations of the rich and complex history and cultural heritage of Central Asia's nomadic and settled populations.

Beyond the Silk Road

arts of Central Asia

The illustrations

Turkmen carpet designs

In 1879, Nicolai Simakoff took part in a Russian scientific expedition to Central Asia, with a special brief to study the industrial arts of the area. While there he completed the original drawings for a folio of 50 chromolithographs, several of which are reproduced in this book. In a commentary on the chromlithographs (translated from the French) Simakoff remarked that Turkmen carpets 'are distinguished by their fine and tight weave, the depth of their colours and the restful harmony of their shading'.

Chromolithograph, drawn by Nicolai Simakoff in Central Asia, 1879, printed in St Petersburg, 1882. 554 x 374 mm. 97/25/33

Simakoff commented that the lower carpet design represents 'scorpions and tarantulas, the inevitable travelling companions of popular traditions'; the drawing at top right records motifs found on bridles, belts and turbans.

Chromolithograph, drawn by Nicolai Simakoff in Central Asia, 1879, printed in St Petersburg, 1882. 554 x 374 mm. 97/25/32

Tekke Turkmen carpet

Very finely woven nomadic flat-weave carpets like this were often dowry pieces. They were used as covers for bedding or to partition the tent, as well as to cover the floor. The cotton weft would have been bought in town.

Wool warp, wool and cotton weft float brocade, made by Tekke Turkmen women in western Turkestan, late 1800s. 3120 x 1850 mm. 85/1900

Yomut Turkmen *khali* (main carpet)

One of the identifying features of Turkmen carpets is the gul, a geometric motif repeated across the central field. The gul used in this rare Yomut rug, which was used to cover the floor of the tent, is called a 'C-gul' because of the small C-shaped motifs it contains. The C-motif is one of a group of archaic Turkic forms that appear in rugs and textiles as far west as the Caucasus and Anatolia.

Wool, symmetrical knots, made by Yomut Turkmen women in western Turkestan, early 1800s. 2480 x 1680 mm. Private collection.

Baluchi prayer rug

The weaver, a nomadic Baluchi woman, has used brilliantly coloured silks for the 'trunks' of the tree motifs in the central mihrab *(prayer niche) and corner spandrels of this rug. The influence of Turkmen design is evident in the* guls *of the wide border surrounding the* mihrab.

Wool warp and weft, wool and silk, asymmetrical knots, made in north-western Afghanistan, about 1900. 1520 x 1030 mm. 96/391/1, purchased with the assistance of the Oriental Rug Society of NSW, 1996

Mushwani Baluchi rug

This village-produced rug, with symmetical knots and lighter-than-usual colours, belongs to a rare group. The three medallion format is typical of later Mushwani rugs, while the curling 'latchhooks' around the medallions hark back to the ancient ram's head motif.

Wool, symmetrical knots, made by Mushwani Baluchi women in western Afghanistan, about 1900. 1880 x 1020 mm. A8358

Khotan floor rug

This is a village or workshop rug, made in or near Khotan, an oasis city on the southern border of the Tarim Basin along which the Silk Road passed. In the mid 1800s, around 5000 carpets a year were produced in Khotan and the surrounding villages. The linear motifs in each corner of the field are stylised Chinese cloudbands.

Cotton warp and weft, asymmetrical wool knots, made, probably by Uighur women, in Khotan, Xinjiang (then eastern Turkestan), 1890s. 1430 x 2650 mm. 94/42/2, gift of Alastair Morrison under the Cultural Gifts Program, 1994

Ningxia floor rug

The saddled-horse motif in the central roundel is rare — a reminder of the ancient tradition of mounted nomadism, which originated in the Mongolian steppes north of China. Carpet weaving was probably established in Ningxia while China was ruled by the Manchu dynasty (1644–1910), whose background was mounted nomadism.

Cotton warp and weft, wool pile, made in Ningxia province, north-western China, about 1840. 1360 x 1950 mm. 94/42/5, gift of Alastair Morrison under the Cultural Gifts Program, 1994

Tekke Turkmen *torba* (small storage bag)

Small bags like this were suspended from the wall of the nomads' yurt (tent) and used to store household items. The major (large) gul is of a type often seen on Tekke torbas, while the minor (small) gul occurs in different forms in a range of Turkmen weavings.

Wool, asymmetrical knots, made by Tekke Turkmen women in southern Turkestan, 1850–1880. 390 x 1175 mm. 87/1526, purchased with the assistance of the Oriental Rug Society of NSW, 1987

Shahsavan storage bag

The design of the large central motif is derived from Turkmen guls, and shows the influence of Turkmen patterns on nomadic weaving west of the Caspian Sea. These bags were used for storage in the tent, and for transporting goods during migrations.

Wool and goat hair, *soumak* (weft wrapping) and complementary weft patterning, made by Shahsavan women of Varamin village region, northwestern Iran (then Persia), about 1900. 370 x 102 x 47 mm. 87/1555, purchased with the assistance of the Oriental Rug Society of NSW, 1987

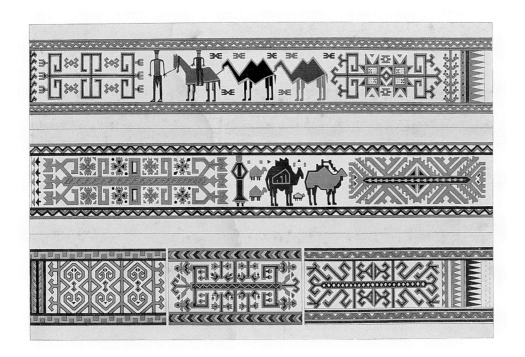

Yomut Turkmen tent band designs

This drawing by Nicolai Simakoff shows a group of Yomut Turkmen tent bands. Nomadic textiles like these, which were made by women, were more likely to include animal motifs than urban textiles, which were made by men. Women were less attached to Islam, which prohibited the artistic representation of people and animals. In Islamic belief only Allah can create life.

Chromolithograph, drawn by Nicolai Simakoff in Central Asia, 1879, printed in St Petersburg, 1882. 554 x 374 mm. 97/25/34

Yomut Turkmen *ak yap* (white tent girth)

This white-ground tent girth is similar to those drawn by Simakoff. It features motifs representing the tree of life and is worked in knotted-pile relief on a plain-weave ground. An ak yap was used in the white wedding tent and was often left in place until the birth of the first child.

Wool, symmetrical knots, woven by Yomut Turkmen women in western Turkestan, about 1890. 13040 x 440 mm. 85/198

Uzbek tent band

Long, narrow tent bands like this one were wrapped around the roof struts of the yurt to maintain an even spacing between the struts. Uzbek rugs and embroideries produced in a nomadic context typically use geometric motifs.

Wool, warp float, probably made by nomadic Uzbeks, about 1900. 5470 x 190 mm. 85/23

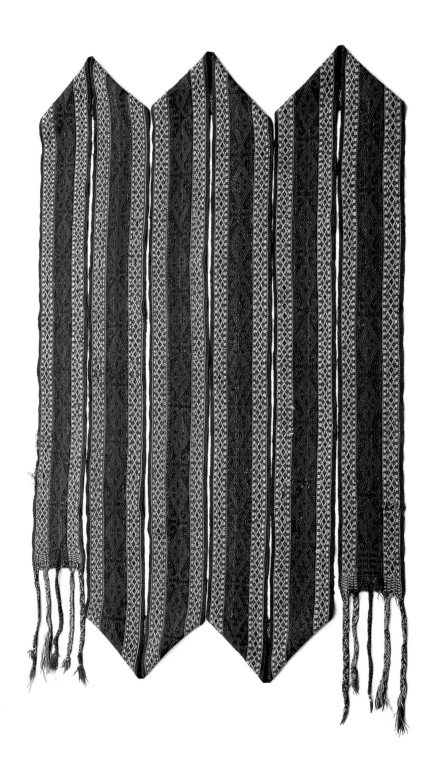

Yomut Turkmen horse cover

Horses were very highly valued by both nomads and townspeople, and were therefore carefully looked after and often decked out in fine trappings. Decorative covers of this type were used at race meetings and other special occasions. The long ends secured the cover round the horse's neck.

Wool and camel hair, warp float patterning, made by Yomut Turkmen women in western Turkestan, about 1900. 1100 x 1600 mm. A9970

Lakai Uzbek camel head-dress

This ceremonial decoration was made by a young Lakai Uzbek women for her dowry. Such head-dresses were worn by the bride's camel during her procession to the white wedding tent. Lakai Uzbek motifs are typically more free-flowing than the dense geometric patterns favoured by the main group of nomadic Uzbeks.

Felt, cotton and horsehair, made and embroidered in Uzbekistan, about 1900. 780 x 480 x 100 mm. 85/22

Tekke Turkmen horse 'jewellery'

These ornaments for a Tekke Turkmen horse comprise bridle, headpiece and neckband. An inscription in Farsi (Persian) on the inside of the neckband translates: 'The work of the master Mohammed Juma, 1901'. The iron bit and brass rings of the bridle are probably later replacements.

Leather, silver, silver gilt, carnelian and turquoise made by Tekke Turkmen in western Turkestan, 1901. 82 x 875 mm (neckband); 240 x 780 mm (headpiece); 280 x 1980 mm (bridle bit and rings). 92/172

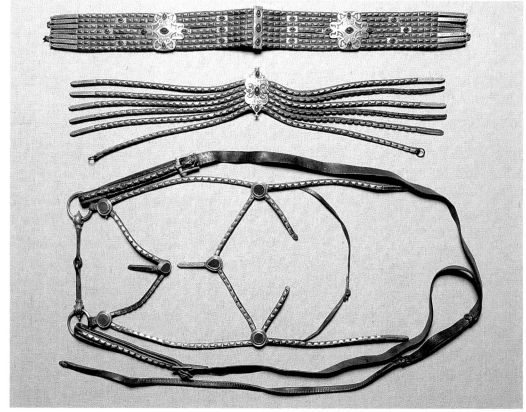

Tekke Turkmen *chyrpy*
(woman's mantle)

Young women wore chyrpys *of dark indigo silk as head coverings on special occasions; married women and the elder women wore yellow and white respectively. The embroidery motifs are stylised tulips and carnations.*

Silk, *kesdi* (interlaced stitch) embroidery, block-printed cotton lining, made by nomadic Tekke Turkmen women in western Turkestan, about 1890. 1160 x 800 mm. A7998

Pashtun woman's dress

The Pashtuns inhabited an area covering most of Afghanistan and parts of northern Pakistan. The triangular amulet motif at the centre front of the dress is to ensure good fortune, as are the round beaded decorations known as gul-i-peron, *or dress flowers.*

Silk and cotton, embroidered with beads, mirror work and braid by Pashtun women in Afghanistan, 1930–1940. 1270 x 1570 mm.
92/1794

Lakai Uzbek
wedding dress and
trousers

*In many parts of
Central Asia, wedding
dresses were made of
purple silk and
elaborately decorated
with embroidery. The
quantity and beauty of
the embroidery
reflected the desirablity
of the young bride who
wore the dress.*

Silk, Russian and Japanese trade
cottons, cross-stitch and
buttonhole stitch embroidery,
made by a Lakai Uzbek woman in
Afghanistan, about 1900. 1070 x
2400 mm.
National Gallery of Australia,
Canberra, 85.263

**Brahvi woman's
pashk (dress)**

*The three ethnic
groups that live in
Baluchistan are the
Brahvis, the Baluchi
and the Pashtuns, all
of whom are mainly
nomadic or semi-
nomadic. The Brahvis
inhabit the mountain
regions south of Quetta.*

Silk and cotton, silk embroidery
and silver ribbon binding, made
in central Baluchistan, Pakistan,
around 1900.
1220 x 1740 mm. A7967-7/1

**Brahvi woman's
pashk (dress)**

*Throughout
Baluchistan, women's
special-occasion dresses
were decorated with
dense embroidery on
the yoke, the cuffs and
the long pointed pocket
at the centre front.
Traditionally, they
were worn with wide
trousers in contrasting
striped silk.*

Silk and cotton, silk embroidery,
and silver ribbon and braid binding,
made in central Baluchistan,
Pakistan, around 1900.
1100 x 1620 mm. A7967-8

Indus Kohistan *jumlo* (woman's dress)

The finest embroidery from this region is worked on items of clothing. The circular motifs, which represent the sun, resemble patterns carved on the rocks in Kohistan, where a sun cult was practised at least 2000 years ago.

Cotton, silk embroidery, block printing, beads, shells, metallic ornaments, made in north-western Pakistan, about 1940.
2110 x 1020 mm. A7120

Indus Kohistan child's hat

Like the women's dresses, children's hats were also densely embroidered and embellished with a wide range of ornaments. These had an 'amuletic' purpose as they were believed to protect the wearer from harm.

Cotton, silk, beads, coins, plastic and pearl buttons, made in north-western Pakistan, 1930–1940.
720 x 150 mm. A10248

Designs for silk ikats

The inspiration for Central Asian ikat patterns comes from a variety of sources, including Turkmen carpet patterns, Timurid tile work and nomadic Uzbek embroidery. This blending of influences reflects the inter-dependence and shared design preferences of nomadic and urban societies in Central Asia.

Chromolithograph, drawn by Nicolai Simakoff in Central Asia (probably Bukhara), 1879, printed in St Petersburg, 1882.
554 x 374 mm. 97/25/ 35

Ikat patterns are often abstract images of the plants and animals of Central Asia, for example, pomegranates and tulips, scorpions, spiders and the ram's horns. The triangular pattern is also common and probably represents the tamar, a protective talisman worn by Turkic peoples.

Chromolithograph, drawn by Nicolai Simakoff in Central Asia (probably Bukhara), 1879, printed in St Petersburg, 1882.
554 x 374 mm. 97/25/36

A Kyrgyz couple in porcelain.

While the Kyrgyz people were principally nomadic, many settled in the villages and towns. The woman is dressed in an ikat-patterned silk robe of the kind made by the Uzbek town dwellers of Bukhara in Uzbekistan (then part of western Turkestan).

Porcelain, made at the Gardner factory in Moscow, about 1890. 261 x 175 mm. A4922

Opposite

Ikat *pardah*
(wall hanging)

The silk workshops of Central Asia produced a range of luxury ikat silks, in which the warp is tie-dyed before being woven. These were used for clothing and to decorate the walls and doorways of town dwellings. Hangings like this were also used as tent walls for outdoor summer occasions.

Silk ikat, made in Bukhara, about 1910. 1450 x 1920 mm. 85/1440

КИРГИЗЫ.

**Woman's *munisak*
(ceremonial outer coat)**

*Outer coats made
of silk ikat, with a
waisted, feminine
shape and open
neckline, like this one,
were worn by women
for important
ceremonial occasions
such as weddings and
funerals.* **Munisak
robes were part of a
woman's dowry and
were laid on the bier
at her funeral.**

Silk ikat, quilted, Russian-printed
cotton lining, woven by Uzbek
men, possibly in Samarkand,
about 1900.
445 x 1440 mm. A7121

Man's *khalat* (coat)

The wealthiest Uzbek men wore up to ten coats at a time on formal occasions, with the very finest—like this one made from bhagmal *(ikat velvet)—on top. These highly complex fabrics were only produced in Bukhara during the latter part of the 1800s. The design motifs include botehs,* ram's horns *and* tamar *(triangular amulets).*

Silk, ikat velvet, embroidered
cuffs, printed-cotton lining, woven
by Uzbek men in Bukhara, about
1870. 1220 x 1425 mm. 85/1439

Caps

Men, women and children from both nomadic and urban groups wore decorative caps. These varied greatly in shape and size, depending on the region and on the age and gender of the wearer, and some served as the base for a turban: (right) is a woman's cap, and (below left and right) caps for a man and a boy respectively.

Man's cap: silk, cotton, metal-wrapped thread, made in northern Afghanistan, about 1940. 215 x 195 x 195 mm. National Gallery of Australia, Canberra, 85.286
Woman's cap: silk velvet, cotton, metal-wrapped thread, made in Bukhara, about 1920. 120 x 190 x 190 mm. H6739.
Boy's cap: silk, cotton, beads, made in northern Afghanistan, about 1940. 110 x 175 x 175 mm. 85.278. National Gallery of Australia, Canberra, 85.278

Embroidery designs

*Across the top and
to the right are drawn
the embroidered borders
of what Simakoff
describes as 'dressing
gowns'. The drawing
on the left is of an
embroidered chamois
leather hunting mitten
with floral motifs
reminiscent of urban
Uzbek suzanis.*

Chromolithograph, drawn by
Nicolai Simakoff in Central Asia,
1879, printed in St Petersburg,
1882. 554 x 374 mm. 97/25/12

61

Bukhara *suzani*
(embroidery)

*Suzanis were dowry
textiles, made by
women in their homes
in the urban centres of
what is now Uzbekistan.
The design was drawn
on strips of cotton cloth,
which were embroidered
by different women of
the family before being
sewn together to make
the whole. Large*
suzanis, *like this
one, were used as
wall hangings.*

Cotton, silk and glass beads,
woven by men and embroidered by
women in Bukhara, about 1800.
1730 x 2340 mm. 92/775

Bukhara *ruijo*
(wedding-bed cover)

This large embroidery was probably originally a ruijo, *or wedding-bed cover, and would normally have had a plain unornamented centre. At one time, however, the centre was filled with brightly-coloured* adras *(silk and cotton fabric), of which tiny fragments still remain. Although identified as Bukharan, the curling tendrils are reminiscent of the melon-vine scrolls on* suzanis *from Samarkand.*

Cotton and silk, chain stitch
worked with tambour hook,
made in Bukhara, about 1900.
3400 x 2330 mm. A9653

63

Timur's architectural legacy

These four drawings are by Simakoff.

Top left and top right:
The exterior and a cross-section of the Gur-Emir mausoleum in Samarkand, where Timur is buried. He died in 1405, on his way to add China to his vast empire.

Lower right:
Drawing of the vault containing Timur's tomb. The stone covering it is the largest block of jade in the world and is thought to have come from the mountains of Khotan in Xinjiang.

Lower left:
Timur was born in 1336 in Char (now Shakhrisabz) on the ancient caravan route to India. He built the massive Ak-Sarai (White Palace) there; the ruins, shown here, remain an intimidating expression of his absolute power.

Chromolithographs, drawn by Nicolai Simakoff in Samarkand and Shakhrisabz in 1879, printed in St Petersburg, 1882. 554 x 374 mm.
97/25/2:5

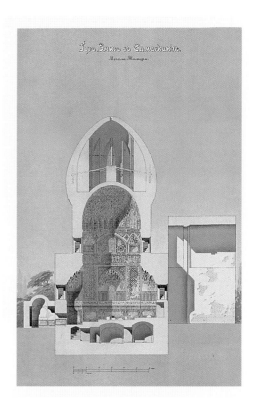

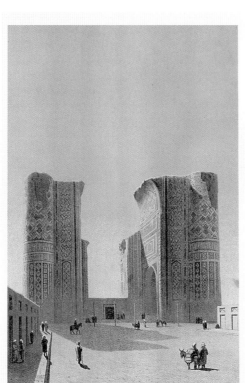

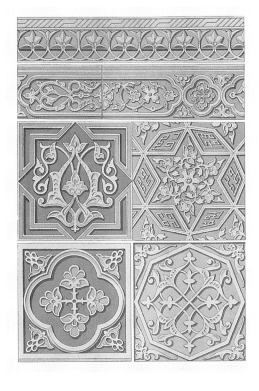

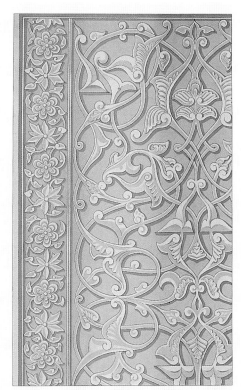

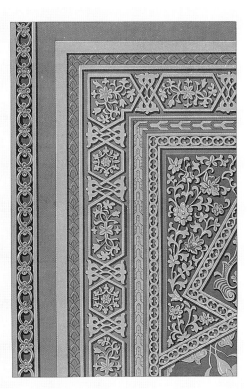

Tomb and throne decorations

Top left:
Simakoff's drawing showing four carved panels from marble tombs in the Shakhi-Zinda cemetery near Samarkand. Across the top are frieze decorations from the tombs of Timur and his parents in the Gur-Emir mausoleum.

Lower left:
Simakoff has drawn carvings on the stone called Kok-tache, which was used as a throne by the emirs of Bukhara. According to tradition, it is the most ancient in the country.

Carved mosque doors

Top right:
Simakoff has drawn the exquisite carving and ivory inlay of a door in the mosque of Khazrete, an islamic holy man who blessed Timur before he set out on a successful expedition against Russia. Timur had the mosque built in his memory.

Lower right:
This drawing shows a mosque door at the Shakhi-Zinda cemetary near Samarkland; the mosque was probably constructed at the end of the 1400s.

Chromolithographs, drawn by Nicolai Simakoff in Russian Turkestan in 1879, printed in St Petersburg, 1882. 554 x 374 mm. 97/25/22,23,26,27

Baked clay ornaments

Here Simakoff has drawn a selection of tiles and ornaments from ancient buildings in Kuldja (Xinjiang), several of which show Chinese influence. At top left and right are mythological creatures that were once used as roof ornaments. Below these is a frieze with the swastika motif that represents the rotation of the heavens.

Chromolithograph, drawn by
Nicolai Simakoff in the Tashkent
museum, 1879, printed in
St Petersburg, 1882.
554 x 374 mm. 97/25/28

Faience tiles at
Shakhi-Zinda

*This drawing is of
tile patterns from
the façade of the
mausoleum of Abou-
Tenghi at the cemetery
of Shakhi-Zinda,
meaning 'the shrine
of the living king',
near Samarkand. Some
of the women and
warriors from Timur's
court in the late 1300s
are buried there.*

Chromolithograph, drawn by
Nicolai Simakoff near Samarkand,
1879, printed in St Petersburg,
1882. 554 x 374 mm. 97/25/10

Wall decoration at Shakhi-Zinda

This drawing is of mosaic patterns on the walls of a mausoleum at the Shakhi-Zinda necropolis near Samarkand. The necropolis was built between the 1200s and the 1600s at the legendary burial place of the Muslim saint Kussam ibn-Abbas, who died in 629.

Chromolithograph, drawn by Nicolai Simakoff near Samarkand, 1879, printed in St Petersburg, 1882. 554 x 374 mm. 97/25/18

Wall decoration at Shakhi-Zinda

This drawing is also of mosaic patterns on the walls of a mausoleum at the Shakhi-Zinda necropolis near Samarkand. The delicate flowers and tendrils that form the mosaics were cut from thin sheets of locally baked and glazed faience and set in mortar.

Chromolithograph, drawn by Nicolai Simakoff near Samarkand, 1879, printed in St Petersburg, 1882. 554 x 374 mm. 97/25/21

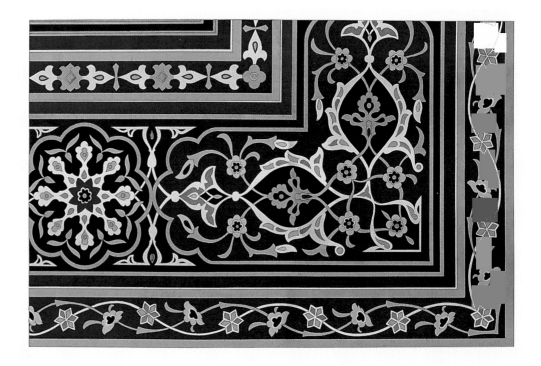

Mosaic designs from
Tilla-Kari mosque

*These drawings are
of tile mosaic patterns
on the outer wall of
the mosque. Tilla-Kari
means 'gold covered'
and refers to the
gilded interior.*

Chromolithograph, drawn by
Nicolai Simakoff in Samarkand,
1879, printed in St Petersburg,
1882. 554 x 374 mm. 97/25/17

69

Tile mosaic fragment

The technique of tile mosaic was developed in Anatolia in the early 1200s, and appeared in Iran and Central Asia in the 1300s. The delicate leafy tendrils of this fragment are similar to those drawn by Simakoff from the mosques and mausoleums of Samarkand.

Glazed earthenware, traces of gilding, made in Iran or Afghanistan, 1400–1600. 180 x 243 x 46 mm. A9636-4

Star tile fragment

The upper half of this eight-pointed star tile with scrolling-leaf pattern has a calligraphic border in Farsi, in naskh *(cursive), script. Star tiles were often used alternately with cross-shaped tiles.*

Painted and glazed earthenware, made in Kashan, 1300–1350. 103 x 195 x 15 mm. A9639-3

Designs of
ceramic forms

*This drawing by
Simakoff features a
selection of earthenware
pots made in Bukhara
in the late 1800s.
Large quantities of
pottery were produced
in western Turkestan
until about this time,
when Russian imports
captured a major share
of the domestic market.*

Chromolithograph, drawn by
Nicolai Simakoff in Bukhara, 1879,
printed in St Petersburg, 1882.
554 x 374 mm. 97/25/6

Designs for majolica

These drawings by Simakoff show the elaborate designs painted on plates from Tashkent.

Chromolithograph, drawn by Nicolai Simakoff in Tashkent, 1879, printed in St Petersburg, 1882. 554 x 374 mm. 97/25/9

Garrus bowl

Typically, the designs on the bowls from the Garrus area of northern Iran feature animal or human figures against a scrolling background. The figure on this example is wearing a short flared skirt and may be a dancer.

Earthenware, champlevé (slip carved) and lead glazed, made in Garrus, ninth century. 70 x 175 x 175 mm. A5201

Nishapur bowl

In the centre of the bowl is a form of the classical Iranian hunting scene. Around the rim are birds and leaves, with highly stylised letters in Kufic script filling the spaces in between.

Earthenware, painted and glazed, made in Nishapur, eastern Iran, ninth century. 80 x 230 x 230 mm. A6019

Iranian lustre vase

Lustre was first used in Egyptian glass in the eighth century. The technique spread to Iraq and then to Iran, where Kashan became a major centre of production between about 1100 and 1400. There was a revival in the mid 1600s at the court of the Safavids, an Iranian dynasty that ruled from 1502 to 1722.

Earthenware with ruby lustre
glaze, probably made in Kashan
in the 1600s.
114 x 114 x 114 mm. A4686

Iranian glass flask

The simple trailing decoration of this utilitarian flask is drawn from the body and encircles the neck. By the mid 1600s there were a number of glass factories in Shiraz, which is thought to be the source of many Iranian glass vessels of the 1700s and 1800s.

Glass, possibly blown in Shiraz,
1700s. 210 x 155 x 45 mm.
85/197

Engraved Iranian
silver beaker

*The beaker is
elaborately decorated
on opposite sides with
a hunting scene, an
image often found on
Iranian carpets. Two
horsemen are shown with
a dog and some birds
against a background
of flowers; one of the
horseman leans over
to catch a deer.*

Engraved silver, made in Iran,
1800–1850. 67 x 67 x 67 mm.
A5829, gift of Mrs A Edgar, 1970

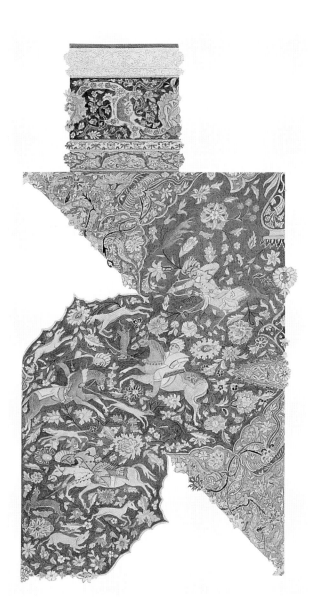

Rug design from Iran

*This design was
drawn by a Russian
artist who fled to Iran
following the Bolshevik
Revolution in 1917.
He set up a business
selling designs to rug
weavers. This design is
for a hunting carpet
with a pattern
symbolising warfare —
an aspect of kingship
in Iran.*

Paper, pencil and watercolour,
painted in Iran, about 1920. 540 x
373 mm. 86/1714

Rug design from Iran

This design, by the same artist as the previous page, is for a medallion carpet, one with a large central motif. The tree is very delicately drawn.

Paper, pencil and watercolour, painted in Iran, about 1920. 324 x 313 mm. 86/1716

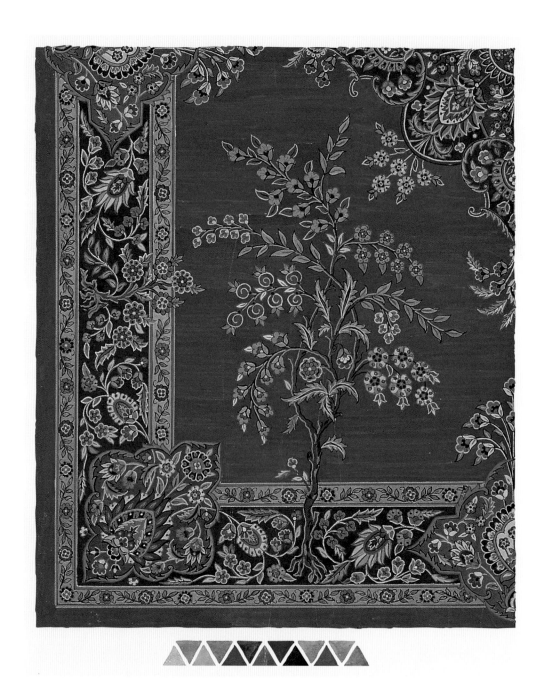

Iranian silk brocade
fragments

*The designers of
Iranian silks from
1500 to 1900 were
more concerned with
decoration than with
botanical accuracy.
These three fragments
feature a variety of
stylised flowers probably
derived from carnations,
irises and daisies.*

Silk, brocade, made in Iran,
between 1700 and 1800.
Top, below left and below right
respectively: 216 x 215 mm; 135 x
115 mm; 87 x 150 mm. A5827-
1:3, gift of Mrs A Edgar, 1970

Decorative painting from Bukhara

In his commentary on the chromolithographs, Simakoff says that ornamentation like this was found everywhere on the ceilings, columns and walls of both public and private buildings, as well as on boxes, mirrors and other domestic objects.

Chromolithograph, drawn by Nicolai Simakoff in Bukhara, 1879, printed in St Petersburg, 1882. 554 x 374 mm. 97/25/19